USING THE CREATIVE ARTS IN THERAPY

Using the Creative Arts in Therapy

The Power of the Arts Experience
to Expand Human Horizons

Edited by Bernie Warren

Illustrations by Roberta Nadeau

CROOM HELM
London & Canberra

BROOKLINE BOOKS
Cambridge, Massachusetts

© 1984 Bernie Warren
Croom Helm Ltd, Provident House, Burrell Row,
Beckenham, Kent BR3 1AT
Croom Helm Australia Pty Ltd, 28 Kembla Street,
Fyshwick, ACT 2609, Australia

British Library Cataloguing in Publication Data

Using the creative arts in therapy.
　1. Art therapy
　I. Warren, Bernie
　615.8'515　　　RC489.A7
　ISBN 0-7099-2779-7 (Pbk)

Published in the USA and dependencies,
Central and South America by
Brookline Books, 29 Ware Street,
Cambridge, Massachusetts 02138

Library of Congress Cataloging in Publication Data
Main entry under title:

Using the creative arts in therapy.

　Bibliography:p.
　Includes indexes.
　1. Arts—Therapeutic use.　2. Movement therapy.
　3. Creative ability.　I. Warren, Bernie, 1953-　.
　RC489.A72U85　1984　616.89'1656　83-24051
　ISBN 0-914797-01-8 (Brookline Books)

Printed and bound in Great Britain

CONTENTS

PREFACE

This book is intended to be a practical introduction to the therapeutic applications of the creative arts. The book is in three parts. In the first, a brief overview of the background, development and philosophy of the therapeutic use of the arts as well as a basic framework for applying the arts as therapy are presented to the reader. Part 2, which comprises the main body of the book, contains chapters from contributing authors, who each address themselves to their specific creative specialisation. The final part contains a scheme for movement analysis, a cross-reference to activities and a Further Reading section.

Each of the authors contributing to the book is first and foremost a practitioner. Throughout this volume we have tried to provide the reader with access to 'track-tested' material, which requires a minimum of training to understand and apply. The intention has been to provide ideas and activities that allow professionals to expand their present knowledge and skills. In so doing, we hope that professionals will increasingly make use of the power of the *arts experience* to help improve the quality of human lives and thereby *expand human horizons*.

It is important to record that although this book is primarily concerned with the therapeutic applications of the arts experience, the authors feel that the ideas, games and activities are valuable not just to those deemed in need of special attention, but to all people — irrespective of age or ability. This is best reflected in the working practices of the contributing authors, all of whom have worked, at different times, in the fields of recreation, education and therapy as well as working as practising artists. More importantly, we see the links between these different areas of application as being essential to the development of our work, complementary rather than mutually exclusive: an important concept in this age of increased specialisation and empire building.

It is important to realise that this book does not provide a panacea for all problems, nor will it make the reader an instant 'arts therapist'. However, it will give an insight into *some* of the techniques, originating in the creative arts, that have proved beneficial in mental health, rehabilitation and special education settings in aiding individuals to gain better control of their bodies and emotions. As an outcome of this increased control over and knowledge of their bodies, they are able to make better use of body, mind and soul and can stamp their own creative thumbprints into the fabric of their daily existence.

This, then, is primarily a practical book, but above all else it is a book about developing human creative expression and enabling all people to be themselves and to express that self to others in a creative and socially acceptable manner. It is this goal that the authors work towards, in the belief that, if we succeed, the improvement in the quality of human life will make arts therapy, and books like this, redundant.

BERNIE WARREN
Calgary, Alberta
May, 1983

ACKNOWLEDGEMENTS

This book is the result of many years of hard work carried out, often unsung, by dedicated professionals working in various parts of the globe. Many of these unsung heroes, without whom the book would never have seen the light of day, are mentioned by contributors throughout this work. There are still many other people who invariably remain unacknowledged yet their contribution to this young and fast-growing body of knowledge is considerable. I would like to take this space to express my sincerest gratitude to all those people with whom I have worked as facilitator, teacher, therapist and friend. The amount I have learnt from you, about the power of the arts experience and of the strength of the human spirit struggling against adversity, is truly immeasurable.

I must also thank Donna Harling, and her husband John and son Sam. Donna has so excellently helped in all stages of this manuscript — typing, editing, layout, etc. — and has never once complained about the unreasonable demands I was making. To John and Sam I extend thanks for allowing Donna to finish our work and more importantly for being our very good friends.

Most importantly, I must acknowledge the support, love and under-standing shown to me by my wife Roberta. Her example of working patiently and with unceasing love and care for all other human beings continues to be the guiding light in my life and in our work together. Finally, I must acknowledge our children, particularly Noelle and Anthony, who have patiently put up with Mom and Dad pounding the typewriter at all hours of the day and night, and yet who understand our work — as long as we don't forget dinner too often.

To all these people, friends, colleagues and 'clients' alike, I dedicate this book.

BW

CONTRIBUTORS

David Stebbing was born in England and has studied Western and Eastern approaches to physical therapy with many highly respected teachers throughout Europe and the USA. He has worked with professional dancers and athletes as well as with physically and psychologically handicapped individuals. David is currently working as a physical therapist from his private practice in Bristol.

Roberta Nadeau was born in the western United States and emigrated to Canada in 1973. She studied psychology and sociology as an undergraduate, graduating *cum laude*. She pursued graduate studies at Purdue University in the sociology of art, and is a painter, who has exhibited her works across Canada, a writer and an arts therapist. She has lectured in the United States, Canada and Europe, and is presently teaching at the University of Calgary and completing her thesis towards a PhD in art therapy.

Bernie Warren was born in England. He initially studied human sciences and later completed extensive studies in dance, drama and music. He has worked as an actor, choreographer and musician. As a community worker, drama teacher and drama therapist he has worked with people of all ages and abilities. Bernie is currently lecturing in acting, developmental drama and drama therapy at the University of Calgary, completing his PhD thesis and working throughout Canada as a freelance arts therapy consultant.

Rob Watling was born in England and received a first in English/folklife studies from Stirling University. Rob has worked as an actor, director, musician, drama teacher, community worker and drama therapist. His experience has been gained with a wide range of disadvantaged, disabled and disturbed individuals. Rob is currently working as a freelance drama therapist/folklorist throughout the United Kingdom and Europe.

R. Keith Yon was born on the island of St Helena and received his professional training in England at the Royal College of Music, the Guildhall School of Music and Drama, and the Central School of Speech and Drama. His work bridges the boundaries between dance, drama and music and he has employed his innovative and eclectic style of working with a broad spectrum of people, covering a wide range of ages and abilities. He was one of three artists working on a three-year project, 'The Arts in the Education of Handicapped Children and Young People', which was sponsored by the Carnegie Trust (UK). Keith is currently a lecturer/tutor in acting-directing, voice-music at Dartington College of Arts, Totnes, Devon.

Part 1

WHY CREATIVE THERAPY?

1 INTRODUCTION

Bernie Warren

The growth of interest in the creative therapies has occurred over a relatively short period of time. This interest has developed as a result of the successes achieved from using the arts in mental health, rehabilitation and special education settings with people whose special needs have identified them as being outside normal society. Many of these successes have been unexpected, certainly not planned and, in some cases, inexplicable. Initially, a handful of pioneering individuals working as arts specialists in the fields of recreation, education and therapy slowly built a strong reputation for the power of the arts experience. Over the last 10 to 15 years, this reputation has been growing slowly but inexorably as more and more specialists work in this area, as more administrators are willing to experiment using the arts in their institutions, and as methodological research is interwoven with anecdotal reports of the effects of the arts experience. As a result, the mixture of experiment, research and anecdote has built a body of ideas, skills and knowledge which has at its core the essence of human existence – a need for each of us, no matter what our age or ability – to reaffirm ourselves and to communicate with others.

The concept of creative therapy is a relatively new one. It is based on the timeless and everchanging relationship between culture, artistic activity and social development. It is perhaps redundant to suggest that the arts and society are inextricably linked and that the health of a society is reflected in the pool of artistic activity the society possesses – and vice versa. Similarly, it may be unnecessary to point out that individual creative output – the individual's right and ability to state 'I am here', 'I am unique' – is a sign of a healthy individual. Yet I believe it is as a result of these relationships that the creative therapies have come to be recognised in the latter part of the twentieth century.

Unlike many societies that preceded us, our technologically advanced industrial society has clearly separated art from life. We have words that allow us to categorise and subdivide art forms. Our society has successfully isolated individuals from artistic creation because art is defined in terms of artefacts, products that can be discussed and criticised – often on the basis of their economic rather than their aesthetic or spiritual contributions to society as a whole. Over the centuries we have created the concept that artistic creation is the responsibility of a few gifted individuals. In so doing, we have denied the mass of society their birthrights: that, as a human being, everyone has the right to make his or her own 'mark' – one that no one else could make. We all have a need to make this 'mark', not because we necessarily wish to be the reminders to a future generation of a long-lost culture – this will always be the prerogative of the few – but because each creative mark reaffirms the self: it says 'I am here', 'I have something to express'.

As the workplace has become increasingly dehumanised and sterile – with fewer and fewer outlets for creative expression, and with an even greater need for outlets for this creative expression to be made available – it is not surprising that the arts have come to be seen as therapy. Slowly, an awareness has evolved that being involved in the process of artistic creation is every bit as important and in many cases more important than the end product. In a world where average individuals are slowly becoming aware of their creative potential, their need to make their mark, it is not surprising that more and more individuals who, by reason of birth, crisis or accident, are unable to take a full part in society are being exposed to the arts experience. The results, in some cases, are literally staggering. Individuals who have been viewed as useless, incapacitated or catatonic have been able to speak, move more freely and in some cases, over a period of time, to take a full and active part in society.

The arts do not stand in isolation and are most definitely not, in themselves, a cure for all ills. However, what the arts can do is, in the individual's act of creation, engage the emotions, free the spirit and make individuals do something because they want to and *not* just because someone decides it is good for them. The arts can motivate in a way possibly no other force can, because it is only through the arts experience, through making a mark that no one else could make, that we express the individual spark of our own humanity.

So, why creative therapy? In essence because all individuals have been removed from their right to indulge in the artistic process of creation and because this process is essential not only to an individual's, but also to a society's well-being. Through reintegration of the artistic process with social experience, the growth of a healthy individual and a healthy society occurs. The way is being led through the use of the arts as therapy. In using the arts with people deemed in need of 'therapy' in mental health, rehabilitation and special education settings, and seeing the reintegration of body, mind and soul and the resulting growth in self-image, self-esteem and healthy social interactions, society as a whole is being handed a mirror, which can reflect what is possible for all its members – if only they are given the opportunity.

Employing the Creative Therapies

The settings in which the creative therapies are used vary tremendously. This diversity reflects the wide application and power of the arts experience. However, it also reflects the diversity of theoretical frameworks[1] and approaches that arts specialists hold, and the wide range of professional conditions within which they must practically implement their skills. It is not the intention of this book to deal in detail with the many and varying philosophical and theoretical frameworks that arts specialists and creative therapists make use of, implicitly or explicitly, in their working lives. However, at the risk of over-simplifying, these can be thought of as a continuum. At one extreme there are mental health and medical models – which often tend towards being rigid and analytical. These models are often based on a guru figure whose followers are a pale imitation of their leader because the guru's system is often based more on charisma and personality than on any repeatable technique. At the other end of the spectrum are human growth and experiential models – these tend towards being loose and unstructured. Many of the people using them work on a 'do what you feel' basis. They often have no system to follow and this is partly because they have had insufficient training to know what techniques to implement when! Even so, it is important to point out that there are extremely well-organised and well-trained professionals working within the experiential models, as well as extremely flexible and eclectic individuals working within the mental health models. What I would advise the reader to be careful of is getting entrenched in a theoretical framework that reduces their role-flexibility as leader.

For individuals beginning to explore this area, part of the problem is in the 'literature'. Writers and speakers on the creative therapies have stumbled over definitions for 20 years. Much of the problem has been caused by attempting to define what creative therapies are, rather than looking at what they do. The emphasis has been on the analysis of the mark produced and how it relates to other bodies of knowlege, rather than on the act of creation itself. As a result, the emphasis has been on looking at the arts as adjuncts to other systems, e.g. nursing care, chemotherapy, psychiatric practice, etc., and as such the arts have been defined and calibrated in their terms. I would like to suggest a switch of focus from the arts in therapy to the therapeutic and often healing power of the arts experience: a switch from assessing the product to indulging in the process. I am not the first to make this suggestion and I am certainly not alone in the conviction that, irrespective of the leader's style of working, it is the act of making a mark — not its effect on an outside professional — that is of value in reintegrating mind, body and soul. The marks may allow the professional an insight into the individual's way of encountering and deciphering the world, but this is really no more than a beacon, a guide to possibilities for the next stage in the process.

I am a great believer in working towards demystification. As already mentioned, the act of creation — of being involved in the arts experience — is both part of our heritage and part of our birthright. There is nothing mystical about it. Each of us can create something unique and meaningful to ourselves. However, in order that we may make use of the arts experience, we do need to understand the techniques and ideas that allow us to be creative. The professional artist will always be looking towards expanding his knowlege and understanding of the skills, techniques and processes that allow him to be creative in his own medium. There is nothing mystical about being creative: all that is necessary is access, understanding and application, i.e. access to materials, teachers, books; understanding of the techniques and ideas; and application of this understanding in a medium that best allows individuals to express themselves, a medium that allows them to be creative.

The problem is that creativity cannot be switched on like a light bulb. You have to have the right power circuit, the right environment in which to create. The starting point for any creative environment is always the leader. You as leader are the most important factor in the direction and development of each individual involved in your session. It will be obvious, but still bears repeating, that the leader sets the tone, provides direction and chooses the material in which individuals will participate. This is true of any leader and is particularly true of the leader employing the creative process in mental health, rehabilitation and special education settings.

In making use of the arts experience in special settings, the leader has to know and understand three basic factors. As leader, you should know yourself, know your art form and know the group you are working with. All of the concepts, ideas and techniques you have learnt will be wasted if you cannot make them accessible to others. Knowledge and understanding of these three basic factors greatly facilitate your group's access to the creative process.

The first factor is probably the most difficult. Very few people honestly know themselves. The external stimuli to which we are all exposed change constantly. We are always having to cope with new pieces of information – some that threaten our beliefs and some that reinforce them. Not everyone can be centred or achieve perfect harmony; however, most leaders can become aware of their strengths and weaknesses, and I believe that this awareness is crucial to being a leader. It is particularly important to be aware of our own vulnerability – the areas that are 'taboo', ways of working that each of us finds difficult, and even groups of people with whom we feel uncomfortable working. If we don't acknowlege these 'vulnerable' areas, it is certain that at some point a group, often a group of children, will discover our Achilles' heel. It is unlikely that any of us will ever be perfect. However, becoming aware of the many facets of our character and working towards increasing the quality and quantity of our positive characteristics and reducing our negative points help to build an awareness of ourselves.

Knowledge of self and security in that knowlege can go a long way to facilitating the controlled release of a group's creative energies. As we become secure in ourselves, so the numbers of the group start to feel secure in our presence. In simple terms, they start to trust us, they start to feel they can be creative, that their endeavours are treated confidentially. As a result, they grow in confidence and self-esteem. I have long been fascinated by my observations of professional colleagues whom I admire. They seem to have the capacity, irrespective of their medium, to extend a circle of energy around the group that acts as a support – as a comforter and friend. It is something I refer to as the leader's 'parental circle' because of its relationship to the support we generally come to expect from our parents. This is something for which I strive.

In working with any group, an understanding of our own working style and favourite medium is particularly important. In addition, knowing different techniques within that medium is essential to the choosing of activities that are suitable to a group's individual and specific needs and abilities. We each have to have experienced the challenge of being faced with a blank piece of paper, or an empty stage, or the request to improvise around a theme in order to understand the problems it can present for others. The root of creation is in experience:

not only experiencing the act of creation, but also allowing that act to recreate past experiences — emotions, events, feelings — channelling them through that creative expression. The artistic process actively engages the senses and the emotions and must be experienced — it cannot simply be reproduced.

Individuals have differing needs. This is as true in terms of artistic and creative expression as it is in any other area. These may change from time to time. At one point a visual medium may be the most conducive to an individual's need to express himself, whereas at another time, for the same individual, singing may be the essential outlet. I am primarily involved in work in the performing arts. However, I am also very visual. My problem is that when working in the visual arts, I seem to have a communication breakdown between my mind and body. Whenever I attempt to work in a primarily visual medium, my hands are unable to create what my mind is asking to be produced. As a result, I am frustrated. Yet the more I work in a visual medium, the easier it becomes for me. This is true for many other people, and thus a slow and patient approach is often necessary. In many cases, individuals need to express themselves in a particular medium, e.g. sound, but do not possess the technical skills to 'say' exactly what they want to. This may be the result of physical restrictions, or simply, as in my case in the visual arts, a limited experience in that medium. Part of the job of a leader is to provide members of a group with the skills, the vocabulary if you like, with which to express themselves in that medium.

Knowing ourselves and our art forms are essentials, but these need to be linked to the needs of our group. We need to structure our sessions so that the group feels secure, that they feel we can and do provide them with the vocabulary and the materials by which they can express themselves. In the next chapter I will address myself to the fundamental question of how these basic ideas can be transformed by the inexperienced leader into practical realities.

Notes

1. For the reader interested in this area, in the first instance I suggest they look at Feder and Feder, *The Expressive Arts Therapies*.

2 PRACTICAL APPROACHES TO THE CREATIVE THERAPIES

Bernie Warren

Preparation and Planning

Very few creative therapists organise and fund their own programmes. Most creative therapists are employed by public health authorities, hospitals, schools, social work departments, rehabilitation centres or other similar public or private institutions, to work within very specific limits with a particular group. It is very important that the basic facts of your working contract are clarified before ever starting work with a group. In terms of contractual arrangements the who, why and what of the agreement are essential. These questions are:

Who will I be working with?
Why am I being employed? and
What am I expected to achieve?

Subsidiary but nevertheless crucial questions are:

When are we expected to meet?
Where do these meetings take place?

The answers to the first three questions will enable you to form some ideas as to *how* the goals set for you and the group might be achieved. The answer to the last two questions will provide a thousand organisational problems, which will make the *why*, the *what* and the *how* more difficult.

The starting point for any creative session is to find out who is in your group. In the initial stages your employer or supervisor will probably present you with a very sketchy outline of the people with whom you are expected to work. In many cases this will provide you with little or no useful information. This is often unintentional and occurs because of an unfamiliarity with the sort of information that will prove useful in running the session. It is important that you find out the information you feel is important. The kinds of basic question that may need to be asked are: How many people will be in the group? How many will be in wheelchairs? Can everyone speak, hear, see? Does anyone have epilepsy? A heart condition? Will I have any professional or voluntary assistance in my sessions? Wherever possible, try to get specific information. To be told someone is suffering an 'emotional disturbance' or has a 'mental handicap' or is 'disabled' is far too general. Try to find out if the members of the group have basically similar abilities and ages. The age of the participants is particularly important, as this will be a factor to be considered when choosing your material. If someone uses vague terms to describe an individual's behaviour, such as 'she exhibits schizophrenic tendencies', try to get him to explain what he means. Also, try to find out under what circumstances these specific behaviours occur. Having said all of this, try to leave yourself room to make your own judgements. It is surprising how happy, co-operative and creative some individuals, whom others see as aggressive, withdrawn or disturbed, can be when given a warm and friendly environment in which they have a chance to express themselves.

The composition of a group – the number, ages and abilities of the individuals within it – is normally worked out over the first two or three sessions. I often only very briefly read the information given to me about the group before the first session and try to 'forget' it, or at least not consciously refer to it, during the running of that session. After the session is over, I compare my perceptions of the group members, based on my observations during the session, with those given to me before I started. I always keep my first sessions simple and fairly undemanding, using activities which are relatively unthreatening and which act, for me, as a gauge of the abilities of the members of that group. These I refer to as diagnostic tools, and in the sections on dance and drama I make reference to some of these activities.

It is also important to be aware that an individual's talents or abilities may lie dormant for a long period, surfacing only when a particular activity engages them. It is for this reason that the contributing authors lay great store on the activities in a session being, above all, enjoyable. There are times when this rule may be broken as some of the material that may surface might be anything but pleasant. However, there is little benefit to be gained from applying the creative therapies if they are viewed in the same light as having to take medication! Enjoyment is an essential motivating factor in the power of the arts experience to enable individuals to overcome their limitations. So often when working with the creative process, an individual will do something that is not only unexpected but also is beyond his previously exhibited capabilities. The arts have that extraordinary power to engage the emotions and so motivate individuals to strive beyond their limits because they are enjoying themselves.

In asking 'Who am I working with', you are slowly able to answer some of the questions relating to the *how* of the contract. However, it is important to know *why* you are working with the group and *what* your supervisor/employer is expecting from you and the group. These may be $64,000 questions, for your perceptions of what you are doing may differ, sometimes drastically, from those of an outside observer. It is here that the creative specialist falls into the recreation, education or therapy debate. There are many creative specialists working under the umbrellas of recreation, education and therapy. Only a small percentage have been trained in the therapeutic application of the arts. Yet many are employed as arts therapists or creative therapists. At the other extreme, highly qualified and professional creative therapists are employed to introduce the arts as recreation within institutions. The problem is that the differences between the three modes of operation are, in some ways, very small but the differences that do exist are important. In general terms it is always important to recognise and state clearly, both to yourself and to your employer, the limits to your training, experience and expertise. This is part of the question 'Why am I being employed?' This question is often clarified by the answer to the question 'What is expected of me?'. It is essential that these are clarified early on, to avoid misunderstandings. For example, an employer may ask you to work as an 'art therapist' and when you stop using craft kits and move towards personal creative expression he will 'slap your wrists' for creating waves; or you may be asked to work as a 'drama games co-ordinator' when what is being asked of you is that you function as a drama therapist. Make sure, in establishing the *why* and *what* of your contract, that you are willing and able to do what is asked of you. There is no point pursuing a contract where you are doing something beyond your experience and training or where it is just not your way of working. In both cases you, your group and your employer are unlikely to benefit from or be satisfied with the situation. The end result is that your contract is likely to be a short and unhappy one.

The *where* and *when* of the contract are possibly the biggest problems facing any leader working within the creative therapies. All too often we meet with our groups too infrequently and in surroundings that do not meet our needs. It is important that you attempt to secure the most suitable room in the building. It is quite likely that 14 other people will be wanting to use that room at exactly the same time. I strongly suggest you do not attempt to share it with them. If you are unable to secure the most suitable room, at least attempt to get one that meets some of your needs. If you are working in the visual arts, you will need a sink – having one 'just down the hall' can be extremely frustrating for you and the group. If you are running a dance-movement session, a carpeted room restricts the possibilities for rolling on the floor. Each of us will have specific needs, but whatever else happens, *try* to get a room that is not a thoroughfare or shared by another group. This is very important in generating a sense of security for your group.

Another factor in establishing the security of a room is to check on its other uses. Try, where possible, to avoid rooms that group members associate with less pleasant activities. Again, this may be impossible; however, it is worth the effort.

A major factor in establishing trust is the continuity and timetabling of your sessions. Avoid requests to change the timing of the sessions in mid-stream. Also, try to avoid time slots that occur just after group members have had a meal. The frequency of your group sessions is often out of your hands, but you should decide what the optimum number of sessions is each week – two or three sessions is probably a good number to aim for. The length of the session will depend on the activities you plan to engage in and the age and ability of your group. As a rough rule of thumb, the visual arts need longer sessions than drama or music, with dance/movement probably requiring shorter but more frequent sessions.

The reality is that you will have very little say in the *where* or *when* of your contract. The room and the time slot for your sessions were probably decided before you were hired. It is important that when you do find yourself in an environment or a timetable that is all but unworkable, you strive towards changing these to meet your needs more adequately. In the meantime, you simply have to make the best of a bad job. Sometimes the knowledge gained from working in unsuitable conditions can be a valuable learning experience. At others it will be a nightmare, which will stay with you all your working life.

The *how* of the contract is the most difficult for me to talk about. I very rarely work with a plan that has been defined in advance. I rely a great deal on my training, past experience and intuition to help guide and plan my sessions. Often I do this 'thinking on my feet'. Essentially what I do is employ activities that I feel comfortable with and that my instinct tells me will meet a particular group's needs at that particular moment in time. The *how* of the contract is esssentially the sum of knowing who you are, knowing your art form and knowing your group. It is about making use of *your* material to meet the needs of *your* group. This will not only mean different things to different people, but will also mean different things to the same person at different times or with different groups.

I strongly recommend that you attempt to gain role-flexibility as a leader. Even if you only work with one group, at different times the needs of the members will be different. For example, sometimes they will want you to be a parent figure telling them what to do, at others they will want you to be an impartial observer, and at still others they will want you simply to be part of the group. It is important that you do not get stuck in an inflexible style, which does not allow room to move. On occasion, what the group wants from you is not what you see as their needs at that time, or the role they cast you in may not be suited to you or you may feel unable to carry it off. It is important that you work within your limits but try to meet the needs you identify in the group.

Working on role-flexibility can be difficult. It is important not to move simply from one extreme to the other. The reins need to be slackened or tightened a little bit at a time – no sudden changes or you will lose control. A group can be overly threatened by a leader whose style ends up being Jekyll and Hyde! One way of learning role-flexibility is to try to get experience of working with other groups. Try to work with other group leaders, observe their style but always remember who you are.

The problem is that leadership styles and role-flexibility are particularly personal. They are learnt and not taught. They become an integral part of a leader's way of working, but they are also dictated by the medium you work in and by specific activities within that medium. Personal creativity will be stifled if you always tell individuals exactly what to do. Yet for some groups, clear, concise and constraining instructions are what is needed in the early stages. Remember, the more directions you give, the less room you allow for personal creativity.

This chapter has been dealing with the basic problems of contract that a leader faces. The contract represents the framework in which you have to operate. A great deal of the contract is initially beyond your control. The content of your session and your style of leadership are uniquely your own. In Chapter 3 I will be outlining some hints for the smooth running of a session – a checklist of ideas that may prove useful.

3 ANNOTATED CHECKLIST OF PREPARATIONS AND PRACTICAL HINTS FOR THE LEADER RUNNING CREATIVE THERAPY SESSIONS

Bernie Warren

Below I have outlined some observations and questions which I feel are important to the running of a successful session of creative therapy. I feel the questions are relevant to anyone leading a creative session, irrespective of their background, experience, style(s) of leadership or the groups with which they are working; however, these factors will obviously affect the answers that each of us gives to these questions. The checklist below reflects my personal concerns, namely: being clear on my responsibilities as leader; treating the people I work with, irrespective of age or ability, as unique human beings; and providing a structure in which people can enjoy themselves, be creative and work towards overcoming the mental, physical or emotional conditions that limit their ability to function adequately within the society in which they live.

The checklist, which is annotated, covers the three basic phases of running a practical session of creative therapy, i.e. before, during and after the session. Many of the points may be obvious to you, some you may think about only occasionally, and others you may not have thought about before. After a while, most of the suggestions and questions that follow become so much an integral part of a leader's way of working that you can strike them from your checklist, as you will be doing them automatically.

Questions to be Answered before Starting the Session

(1) Who am I working with?

(a) How many people will be in the group? Will this number be constant?
    Often this number will fluctuate. Someone may be ill, need to to go to surgery, X-ray, dentist, hairdresser, or a million and one other places. Be patient and be prepared for these changing numbers.

(b) What are the ages of the group members? Are they more or less the same age?

(c) What are the *abilities* of the group members? Can they all walk? Is there a common link between members of the group? For example, have all the group suffered a stroke?

It is always important to plan specifically *for your group. No two groups are ever exactly the same, but obviously experience gained with similar groups is very valuable. The key is in choosing activities which allow group members to succeed.*

(d) Do I know everything I need to know about the members of this group? For example, are any members of the group on medication which will limit their creative potential (i.e. heavy sedation)?

It is highly unlikely that you will know everything you would like to know before the start of the first session. You will almost certainly gain valuable information from your own work.

(2) What are my Responsibilities as Leader?

(a) In what capacity am I being employed? Drama teacher? Recreation instructor? Drama therapist? Play leader? Arts therapist?

(b) What am I expected to do with the group? Is my job to engage the group directly in creative activities, or am I employed to seek actively to change specific behaviours?

(c) If my job is to change specific behaviours, what is the time frame in which I am expected to do this? Is this time frame realistic?

(d) Am I capable of carrying out what has been asked of me?

(e) Do I need to renegotiate my 'contract'? That is, what I am expected to achieve with the group through my creative medium? (see also 'Questions to be Answered after the Session is Over'.)

If your job description and your duties clash, there is a need to clarify exactly what is expected of you. There is also a need for you to make clear to your employer/supervisor your skills. There is a vast difference between accepting a challenge and misrepresenting your abilities. Often you may need to re-educate your employer/supervisor about why you work creatively and what you see your skills being in relation to your group.

(3) Pre-session Planning

(a) When is the session timetabled? How often do I see the group and for how long each session?

(b) Do the group members know where and when we meet? Do the other professional staff who work with them also know this information?

Often you will have no *say in the frequency or timing of your sessions. If your sessions are too long, allow time for simply talking and being with the members of the group. If the session is too short, allow yourself time before and/or after the session to be with the group. This unstructured 'talk time' can often be essential to an individual developing trust in you. It also provides a time to share what has been happening in the group's lives.*

(c)   What space do I need to work in? Does the space I have been allocated meet these needs? For example, does it have running water and a sufficient number of chairs? Is it comfortable? If not, how can I make do with the space I've been given?

It is essential that you make clear to the person dealing with timetabling and administration exactly what your needs are. Demand the impossible – go for what you would want ideally and barter from there!

(d)   Will I have any assistants? Will they be volunteers or professionals? Do they know the group members? Do they know my way of working? Do they know what my goals are?

It is not unusual for your assistants to know the group better than you. This can be an extremely valuable asset. Make use of these people. Wherever possible, run workshops for them prior to working with your group. Take them into your confidence, share ideas and information with them. One word of caution – always *remember that, no matter what happens, you are in control (sometimes difficult to get across to some people).*

(4) Planning the Session

(a)   Given all the information I now have, how can I best achieve my goals?

These may be different from those suggested by your employer/ supervisor.

(b)   What activities will best match my strengths with the perceived needs of the group and their abilities?

(c)   How much structure do I need to provide for the group so they can actively engage in these activities?

Much of this may have to be left open until after your first session. Try to provide, in the first few sessions, activities, structures and language systems that allow you room to change direction without breaking the trust and security you are developing.

(d)   What equipment will I need? Is this to be provided for me? Am I expected to take my own art supplies? Tape recorder? Musical instruments?

Many creative specialists always carry their own materials around with them. It is perhaps the one way of ensuring you have exactly the materials you need. Try to be reimbursed, or given an equipment budget to cover these costs.

(e)   Is the room with which I have been provided still going to function for me? Do I need to negotiate another space?

This may be difficult, but always try to get the room that suits you. If you need a sink for art work, or a piano, or a clean space to roll on, keep on pressing for your needs. It may be difficult explaining to someone unfamiliar with your creative medium why you need these facilities – but keep on trying.

Points to Look for and Questions to Ask Yourself during the Session

(1) Immediately prior to the Session

(a)   Is all the equipment I need for this session here?

(b)   Are all the group members here? What is the general mood of the group? Is it in keeping with my plans for this session?

In some cases you may want to keep that mood. In others, you may wish to dispel it. Either way, you may feel the need to change your plans. Flexibility of approach is one of the keys to successful and creative leadership.

(2) Running the Session

(a)   Did I introduce myself? Do the group know why I am here and what we will be doing together? How do they react to this?

(b)   Do I know the individuals in this group?

Every group is different. Every individual in every group is unique. Each makes their mark differently. The medium in which they are most creative differs. Name games, sharing information and allowing group members to feel they are part of the group's decision-making process is essential. All too often, leaders do not even consider asking a group what they would like to do.

(c)   Am I warming up the group for the activities to come?

The warm-up sets the tone for the rest of the session. If it is to be 'physically strenuous', it is important to warm up the joints and the muscles. If imagination is to be the focus of the session, exercises to warm up the imagination will be needed. If there is lethargy at the beginning of an active session, it's very unlikely that your group will be prepared to expend any energy without being coaxed.

(d)   How are group members responding? Who is outgoing? Who is shy?

(e)   Am I introducing the activities in a way that people can understand? Am I working at their pace?

(f)   Am I providing the right amount of structure to allow the group to be creative?

(g)   Am I meeting the individual needs of the group? Am I aware of changes occurring in these needs throughout the session?

Throughout the session, no matter how actively involved you are, you must be sensitive to the needs of all the group. This requires tremendous amounts of concentration, and, in particular, paying heed to all the observed behaviours of the group. Careful note should be made of whether you are using language that the group understands. You may need to vary the language level, i.e. complexity of words; the language system – the way you put sentences together; and will certainly need to reinforce your requests/commands with gestural clues – so as to communicate with all the group's members. Another point to watch out for is – not only working at the group's pace, but also always starting an activity at the beginning and not where you left off with this or some other group. As to the structure, you will have to sense if you need to let go of the reins or pull them in even more. This is something one learns with experience and unfortunately experience can not be gained from any book.

(h)   Am I simply filling the session up with 'busy time'?

(i)   Am I enjoying myself?

If you are not enjoying yourself, it is almost certain that no one else will be. However, be careful that you are not the only person enjoying yourself. Remember who the session is for; it is often important to remind your assistants about this too. If you do get caught in a 'playing to the crowd' mentality, the session may degenerate into 'busy time': a lot happening, but nothing being done.

(j)   How can I end this session on a positive but relaxing note?

Lying on the floor, listening to tranquil music, gentle rocking in pairs, telling the group a story while they lie on the floor with their eyes closed, working with a parachute – are all examples of ends to a session which are both relaxing and positive.

(3) Immediately after the Session

(a)   Does everyone know when the next session will be? Do I need to send notes back with certain individuals?

(b) Has everyone got all the possessions that they arrived with?

(c) Have I got everything I came with?

(d) Have I checked all the lights are out? Water turned off? Is the room in more or less the same state I found it?
This is particularly necessary as janitors and cleaners are possibly the most important professionals we come in contact with!

Questions to be Answered after the Session is Over

(1) Evaluating the Session

(a) How did the group respond? To me? To my material? To other members of the group? Was this as I expected?

(b) How did I feel about the session, e.g. good, uneasy, bad? Can I pinpoint a reason for this? The room? My presentation? My contract? My material?

(c) Did I meet any of my goals this session? Did I identify new goals during the session?

(d) Have I made a written note of my observations and feelings about the session yet?
I feel it is extremely important to keep written records. These should not just be a clinical account of what happened. They should include observations of what went on, how the group members participated and how you felt the session went. I have always kept a journal of every session I have ever run and these have proved invaluable – not only during the sessions, but also after the sessions have finished.

(2) Planning for the Next Session

(a) Am I basically on the right track? Do I need to change my approach? My material? My medium? Do I need to renegotiate my contract?

(b) Who are the individuals in the group who need special attention? How can I best meet these needs without disturbing other members of the group?

(c) What shall I do next time? How can I link it to what we have already done so that it builds on these experiences?
The answers to these questions will be extremely specific. The only observation I will make is that it is essential that you link your material to your own personality and to the personalities in your group!

(d) Have I made sure that I have scheduled time for me to have a

break between sessions?
In the long run it is essential that you timetable 'space' for your-self to replenish the energy you have expended. As my wife, Roberta, often says, 'You cannot pour from an empty cup.'

The most important thing to remember is that everyone in the room is a human being. You, your assistants and the members of your group all have good and bad days. All of you will experience frustration and elation, failure and success. If you can bear that in mind, you will be a long way down the road not only to allowing the people you work with the joy of the arts experience, but also to standing a good chance of allowing them to expand their own human horizons.

The rest of this book is devoted to practical activities that will allow you to share the power of the arts experience with others.

Part 2

PRACTICAL ACTIVITIES

4 FOLKLORE/RITUAL AS A BASIS FOR PERSONAL GROWTH AND THERAPY

Rob Watling

Folklore is that part of any culture which is transmitted by word of mouth or by custom and practice. It includes folk literature (folktales, poems, songs, dramas), folksay (proverbs, riddles, rhymes, dialect), customs and beliefs, music, dance and ethnography (the study of arts, crafts and the manufacture and use of artefacts). It is important to realise that modern industrialised societies have folklore in the same way as American indians or Australian aborigines. Nor should we think of folklore as 'the things our grandparents used to do' for it is a vital part of the way all societies operate. There is as much folklore in the city as in the jungle.

This traditional material, wherever it is found, belongs to the people who use it. They have devised it when they have wanted it, transmitted it from generation to generation, adapted it when necessary, and discarded it when they have no further need for it. It is constantly changing, and almost infinitely variable. It is functional (as we shall see later) and it has stood the test of time. Traditional societies do not have drama therapists, but neither do they seem to be snowed under with the sorts of problems that we, as therapists, are helping our clients to tackle. Without making a romantic appeal for some sort of return to a simpler, more ethnocentric way of life, I believe that we do have important lessons to learn from tradition and I have found my working knowlege of folklore invaluable to me in many of my sessions. It has served both as a source of material and as part of a theoretical model of what happens in the therapeutic setting. But before we look at some of the applications of folklore we need to know a little more about the subject.

Many of the early folklorists, working in the nineteenth century, concentrated purely on collecting large quantities of material. They wanted to list the things people did – the songs they sang, the rituals they performed, the tales they told or the tools they used. Collections of this information were compiled but it was some years before people began to realise that the material was not enough by itself. It was not sufficient to know that 'Waly Waly' was a Scottish ballad. They began to ask who sings it, to whom, where and when? Where was it learnt, how is it remembered and why does it exist at all? Is it just a sad song? Is it a cautionary tale? Is it a record of an important event in a society unable to perpetuate its history with pen and ink? This new generation of students wanted to know about the *context and the function of the living material*. It is context and function that interest us, too.

Folklore has been shown to have an enormous range of functions. A simple folktale can, in certain contexts: relate the history and wisdom of a society; reinforce custom and taboo; teach skills by example; explain the mysteries of the universe and man's place within it; amuse and entertain; offer solutions to personal and practical problems . . . the list can be made very long and other types of material can have as many varied functions. Here are four particular examples:

The Anang in Nigeria, like many other African tribes, use proverbs as a central part of their judicial system. Plaintiff and defendant quote proverbs (widely used as the embodiment of tribal wisdom) to support their cases.[1]

In China, while the tyrannical Chin Shih Whang was having the Great Wall built, folk-songs emerged as an expression of the people's feelings − their grief at the death of so many labourers, their fury at the enforced break-up of so many families as men were sent away to build the wall, their opposition to the capital punishment of those who refused to go. Popular protest songs, passed on by word of mouth, are still around today.[2]

The Inuit of North America will sometimes have a singing dual to settle a dispute in a non-violent way (violence is not welcome in the close confines of a winter settlement). The combatants sing songs at each other with the intention of ridiculing their opponent into submission. They channel their antagonism into a functional, conclusive ritual.[3]

In Norse mythology, on the other hand, combatants will indulge in an insult-flinging competition as a precursor to a battle. Here the idea seems to be to goad your partner into action and to prepare yourself for victory.

This notion that folklore can and should be studied in terms of its context and function is central to us if we wish to apply traditional material to a therapeutic setting. We could sit in a circle and sing war chants, we could perform traditional Swiss dances, tell each other Russian folktales or play Welsh street games. But as therapists we need to understand what it is we are doing and with whom. We, too, need a firm notion of the context and function of our material and the way in which these elements relate to each other. This relationship can be illustrated by a simple diagram, in which the shading denotes areas

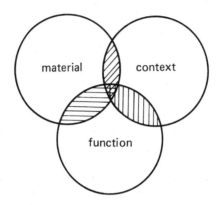

of change and mutual influence. When any one of the variables in the diagram alters, it may affect one or both or neither of the others. Take, for example, the game of 'London' described later in this chapter. As it is found in tradition, being played by a group of children, this material is 'just a game'. Its context might be described as a backstreet game, played by friends in their leisure time. The function of the game appears to be fun; something to pass the time; perhaps a chance to consolidate friendship or to practice competitiveness. If we change the context by playing this game in a therapy session, what else do we change? Perhaps we change nothing, as we can play this game for its own sake. But we could decide to use this game with a group who need to develop gross motor control. Now we could add the function of teaching people to stop quickly and to control their balance to our list. It is still the same material but now with new context and function. We can go further (as in the 'collective' version of the game that I describe) and change the rules of the game. It is no longer 'every man for himself' but an exercise in co-operation. Context, function and material are variables for us and the group to alter as we wish.

Folklore is a powerful, accessible, adaptable source of material, which offers us insights into the way people act and interact with each other and the environment. Once we understand some basic principles of the way in which it operates, we are in a position to apply some of this material in a therapeutic way. The rest of this chapter outlines some practical ways this can be done, with particular reference to traditional games, folk narratives and simple rituals.

Traditional Games[4]

I have tried to suggest games of different types in this section, varying from the fast and furious to the slow and contemplative. All of them, I hope, contain the essential element of fun referrred to in other parts of this book. By way of explanation, I have used the term 'It' to describe the player who is working against the rest of the group, usually in an effort to catch them. 'It' is often called 'He', 'Her', 'On' or 'On it' in Britain.[5]

Stick in the Mud

This is an excellent game with which to start a session and one which is always a great favourite. It is often called 'Sticky Glue', 'Release', 'Ticky Underlegs' or 'Underground Tag'.

One player is 'It' and chases the others. Anyone 'It' touches must stand with their arms outstretched and their legs apart — they are 'stuck in the mud'. They must stand still until another player frees them by crawling between their legs. They may then run off again. Sometimes players are required to call 'SOS' or 'Release' while they are stuck in the mud. 'Its' job is to get everyone stuck in the mud, which is by no means easy. I quite often have two 'Its' to make the game less frustrating. The first and/or the last people to be caught are 'It' next time round.

This is a fast, energetic game involving a variety of movement and body shapes, basic teamwork and usually quite a lot of noise. It can be useful as an exercise for those needing to develop simple spatial awareness and can easily be adapted for different ability groups. Slowing the game down to a walking pace can be useful, so can changing the 'freeing' act for a simpler manoeuvre. Some people find it easier to stand near a wall when they have been tagged and to hold up an arm or a stick to form an archway. They are released when someone goes through the arch (this is sometimes called 'Tunnel Touch'). Alternatively, the game can be made more demanding: players must move around the room in a particular way; you must crawl backwards through a captive's legs to free them; play the game linked to a partner so that pairs of people have to crawl through two sets of legs. As ever, the possibilities are endless and can be matched to the abilities of your group or used to lead them into new areas of movement and activity.

Sun and Frost

This is a version of Stick in the Mud played in Stornoway in the Isle of Lewis and was collected by the Opies from an eleven-year-old girl who said,

> 'You all stand in a row and one person picks the nicest face for the sun, and the rest that's left they all put on ugly faces and pick the ugliest (for the frost). The people that's left all go out and the frost goes after them and if they're caught they have to stand still till the sun tips them and they will get free. That's how you play the Sun and Frost.'[6]

The obvious symbolism in this game can be of use to many groups over and above the physical benefits of movement. I have sometimes extended the idea and asked the Frost to 'really freeze' the players and the Sun to thaw them out with a warm hug and a nice sigh. There are many other traditional games where quite intimate body contact is perfectly acceptable, and they can be used, among other things, for the recognition of body parts.

London

A game with incredibly wide circulation, this is known in various parts of the world as 'Red Light, Green Light', 'Ochs am Berg', 'Eins zwei drei — sauer Hering!', 'Uno, due, tre, stella', 'Grandmother's Footsteps' or simply 'Freeze'.

Originally played across a street or a yard, 'It' stands facing a wall with all the other players on the opposite side of the road. The object is for them to creep up and tap 'It' on the shoulder, but at any moment 'It' may suddenly turn round. Anyone 'It' sees moving (even a hand) is sent back to the start. 'It' may look round any number of times but is often required to count silently to ten between each go or to say a short phrase in his head to give the others a chance. The first player to get right across is the next 'It'.

This game is immensely popular and is nearly always played with complete equanimity. This has much to do with the quality of the 'It' role, for 'It' has considerably more control over the proceedings than in chasing and tagging games. This is one of those rare games where 'It' is the coveted role, but has the additional advantage that everyone else can feel that they are succeeding – even the ones who are sent to the back to the start, for they are now hidden by the people in front of them and can move forward more quickly. A headstrong dash for the finish is rarely successful and the quiet individual can often win by stealth. I have seen many players delight in the attention they receive in being sent back over and over again. It is rare for players to accuse each other of cheating or to refuse to accept 'Its' verdict.

In therapy the game is useful in a number of ways. It is fun, of course, and can relax a group very quickly, helping to create a good working atmosphere. It improves concentration and alertness and can be used to develop body awareness, balance and gross motor control. Faced with a group of adolescent boys who were having difficulty making group decisions and acting co-operatively, I developed a variation we called 'Group London'. There was still one 'It' but the rest of the group had secretly to select one of their number as the one they wanted to 'make it' to the other side. Their job was to help him get across by shielding him from view, or by 'sacrificing' themselves and drawing 'Its' attention away from him. The dynamic of the game changed dramatically and I have used it on a number of occasions as a link between more self-centred games and exercises to develop group cohesion.

As a widely known game London also serves as a good example of another benefit of traditional material. Many people playing these games will remember their own variant and can make a positive contribution to the session (something they might otherwise find difficult). I have run whole sessions with all the activities suggested by group members from their own repertoire of traditional material.

Muk

This game is part of the traditional winter activity of the Inuit (Eskimo). The players sit talking and joking in a circle with 'It' in the centre. Suddenly 'It' will say 'Muk' (the Inuit word for silence) where-upon no one must make a sound. 'It', however, is allowed to tell jokes, fool around, pull faces or whatever until someone breaks the muk. That person is then given a comic name (traditionally the name of an animal) and either replaces the 'It' or joins them as part of a growing team of animals who will eventually descend on the last silent member of the group.

Ostensibly a game about the breaking down of barriers between individuals (one of the social functions for the Inuit), in our society this game can easily become an exercise in reinforcing these barriers. This is particularly likely in a group where people have problems with communication and self-presentation and 'It' can quite quickly feel threatened and ostracised. The therapist is at liberty to make capital out of this (perhaps moving on to more intensive work) or to defuse the situation by having more than one person in the middle. You may wish to stop the game when there are still three or four people in the outer circle to avoid the group applying all its coercion on one individual, but this last breakdown can have a unifying effect on the group and restore the element of fun.

Irish Wake Games[7]

The traditional Irish funeral was a fascinating mixture of solemnity and joviality for, in common with the funeral rites of many cultures, it served as an opportunity not only to pay respect to the dead but also to celebrate life and the living. Most, if not all, of the amusements have now been separated from the modern Irish wake, largely in response to the disapproval of the church, but we still know enough about them and the way they were played to understand at least some of their functions in this context.

The wake itself, where relatives and neighbours would watch over the coffin until the funeral, was partly a chance for people to express their respect and to show their mourning. It also served to guard the coffin overnight from evil influences — which could mean spirits, the devil, body-snatchers or all three. There would be much drinking and eating at a wake and there was as much singing and dancing as at any other Irish gathering. But there were also these games to help people stay awake and relatively sober at their task. There were riddles, trials of strength and dexterity, tricks of all sorts and forfeits galore, all acting as a confirmation, a celebration of the living at a time of deep respect for the dead.

Pig in the Sty

One person (traditionally a woman) stands in the middle of a ring of players who link arms as securely as possible. Outside the ring is another player (usually a man). His job is to kiss the girl in the middle either by reaching over the ring of linked players or by forcing his way through. (At this stage the ring may decide to let the girl escape and to keep the man prisoner.) All the other players try to frustrate the man's attempts until he is successful or resigns.

This game can be used in a number of ways: to act as a warm-up, to channel physical aggression, to develop co-operative energy, to break down barriers to physical contact (which can here be intimate but safe), to illustrate rejection and corporate disapproval or to promote a discussion on traditional sex roles. The game can easily be adapted by encouraging different techniques: use no hands; everyone has eyes closed; tickling is allowed; use persuasion to gain entry into the circle; cheat; etc.

Do the Opposite

This was a common amusement at the wakes and one which I have found popular with all sorts of groups, the object being to trick people into making simple mistakes. Two players, for example, hold a scarf between them and are told to do the opposite of any instruction you give them. You tell them to hold it tight and they should let go, you tell them to pick it up and they should leave it alone, you tell them to keep it away from other people and they should give it to a new couple. Any mistake (and there are many) is punished with a forfeit — I use a hit on the head with a balloon. The game is, once again, infinitely variable and can easily be adapted to the abilities and concentrative powers of most groups. It is great fun to watch, for humour is a great leveller. Once everyone has been fooled (including you, for the therapist should join in whenever possible in these games) the whole group has greater access to each other as individuals.

Cumulative Games

Another adaptable concentration exercise is the cumulative memory game. The first player in a circle, for example, says 'I went to market yesterday and bought a cow.' The second player says, 'I went to market yesterday and bought a cow and a sheep.' The third says, 'I went to market yesterday and bought a cow, a sheep and a sack of corn.' And so it goes on with each player adding something new to the list. Again it must be used at an appropriate level for the group. Some groups will be able to go round the circle several times without making a mistake; for others it will be a considerable achievement if they can repeat what their neighbour has just said. Be prepared to use memory aids (pictures, mime, sound-clues) and look for ways to develop additional skills in the same game (recognising the idea of 'sets of things', counting, non-verbal communication, etc.).

Traditional Narratives

Story-telling can be a fulfilling experience in its own right. Traditional tales, poems, ballads and dramas (as well as some modern literary ones) embody all sorts of wisdom: teachings, history, parables and advice; for the folk narrative is often the living encyclopedia and life-manual of the non-literate society. Even the simple act of being a member of an audience can be calming and nearly everyone loves to be told a story. We need not limit ourselves to straightforward tale-telling sessions, however useful they may be, but can reinforce their meanings and messages in a number of ways. It can often be valuable to ask groups to externalise their reactions to a narrative in discussions, in paintings and sculptures, in a dance perhaps, or by acting out some of the scenes. Ask your group to project their ideas of what happened before the start of the story and what happens afterwards. Use the narrative and its accessibility as a platform for all sorts of expression and discovery.

Since it is often the hero or protagonist with whom we are meant to identify, who encounters our own predicament and symbolises ourselves, it can often be valuable to use a traditional narrative as the basis of a guided fantasy. In this exercise each member of the group listens to the story and acts out the part of the central character as the adventure unfolds: doing what the protagonist does; 'seeing' what he sees; 'feeling' what he feels; and learning (often intuitively) what the hero learns. A whole wealth of human experiences can be fed into each group member, who need not be self-conscious about the quality of their performance as it is directed inwards rather than out at an audience.

Ritual and the Therapy Session

Rituals have always formed an important part of the collective and individual actions of people throughout the world. From the indian dance to the swinging of Catholic incense, from the blood sacrifice on a new boat to the 'wetting of a baby's head' in an English pub, from the rain dance to the children trying not to step on the cracks of the sidewalk, rituals are anchors of certainty in a precarious sea. At the moment of ritual we know exactly where we stand.

There are many times when a client or a group need, in exactly the same way, to know where they stand: at the start of a session; when a new member joins the group; when a group member faces a crisis or shares a moving experience; at the close of the session. At moments like these it can sometimes be helpful for a group to use some sort of ritual as a collective expression of a shared experience. The predictability of ritual can help to take the slightly frightening edge off a session. There is one regular weekly group I attend whose members are comforted not just by our occasional use of simple ritual but by our predictable, almost ritualistic use of traditional games as a mainstay of our work together. They know what to expect from the sessions and can learn to understand their place within them.

But a word of warning. I have been a member of several workshops and sessions where a ritual has been artificially imposed on a group. 'We are now going to show our unity for each other's feelings and experiences by joining with everyone in the room and silently communing with each other. . .', said the therapist. Unfortunately it was obvious that the group wanted, on this occasion, to reflect individually on their own experiences. They were a square peg being tapped remorselessly into a round hole. Any worthwhile ritual expression must have its roots in the nature of the therapeutic experience. It is material that must be appropriate to the context and suited to its intended function. It is not hard to develop rituals with and for a group, but we must insist that our modern-day material takes a lesson from its traditional counterpart. All creative therapy must work as an expression, not as an imposition. And folklore, the carrier of wisdom, faith, joy and learning for thousands of years, has never successfully been imposed on anyone.

Notes

1. Messenger, John C. Jr. (1959) 'The Role of Proverbs in a Nigerian Judicial System', *Southwestern Journal of Anthropology*, *15*, 29-37, reprinted in

Dundes' *The Study of Foklore*, pp. 299-307.

2. Wang, Betty (1935) 'Folksongs as Regulators of Politics', *Sociology and Social Research*, *20*, 161-6, reprinted in Dundes' *The Study of Folklore*, pp. 308-13.

3. Burkett-Smith, K. (1971) *Eskimos*, Copenhagen, pp. 59, 164, 173.

4. Still the definitive work on the traditional children's games from England and Wales is the Opies' *Children's Games in Street and Playground*. There is an enormous wealth of material in the Opies' works, including versions of the first three games in this section.

5. Gump, Paul V. and Sutton-Smith, Brian (1955) 'The It Role in Children's Games', *The Group*, *17* (*3*, February), 3-8, reprinted in Dundes' *The Study of Folklore*, pp. 329-36. This article contains a fascinating preliminary discussion on some of the possible functional applications of selected 'It' games.

6. *Children's Games in Street and Playground*, p. 111.

7. For a fuller study of this material in context, see Sean O'Suillebahn's *Irish Wake Amusements*.

Suggested Reading

General Folklore

Brunvand, J.H. *The Study of American Folklore*, 2nd edn (Norton, New York, 1978)

Dorson, R.M. (ed.) *Folklore and Folklife, an Introduction* (University of Chicago Press, Chicago, 1972)

Dundes, A. (ed.) *The Study of Folklore* (Prentice-Hall, NJ, 1965)

Traditional Games

Brewster, P.G. 'Children's Games and Rhymes', *The Frank C. Brown Collection of North Carolina Folklore*, vol. 1, pp. 29-219 (Durham, North Carolina, 1952)

Brown, W.K. 'Cultural Learning through Game Structures: a Study of Pennsylvania German Children's Games', *Pennsylvania Folklife*, *22* (1974) 2-11

Eckhardt, R. 'From Handclap to Line Play', *Black Girls at Play: Perspectives on Childhood Development*, pp. 57-101 (Southwest Educational Development Laboratory, Austin, 1975)

Ferretti, F. *The Great American Book of Sidewalk, Stoop, Dirt, Curb and Alley Games* (Workman Press, New York, 1975)

Newell, W.W. *Games and Songs of American Children* (Dover, New York, 1963) (first published 1883)

Opie, I. and P. *The Lore and Language of Schoolchildren* (Oxford, Oxford University Press, 1959)

Opie, I. and P. *Children's Games in Street and Playground* (Oxford, Oxford University Press, 1969)

Orlick, T. *The Cooperative Sports and Games Book* (Readers and Writers, London, 1978)

O'Suillebahn, S. *Irish Wake Amusements* (Mercier, Cork, 1969)

Traditional Narratives

Bettelheim, B. *The Uses of Enchantment* (Penguin, Harmondsworth, 1979)

Buchan, D. *A Scottish Ballad Book* (Routledge, London and Boston, 1973)

Briggs, K. *A Sampler of British Folk Tales* (Routledge, London and Boston, 1977)

Child, F.J. *The English and Scottish Popular Ballads,* 5 vols (reprinted by Dover, New York, 1965)

Clark, E.E, *Indian Legends of Canada* (McLelland and Stewart, Toronto, 1960)

Dorson, R. *Buying the Wind* (University of Chicago Press, Chicago, 1964)

Friedman, A.B. *The Penguin Book of Folk Ballads of the English-speaking World* (Penguin, Harmondsworth, 1977)

Luthi, M. *Once upon a Time: on the Nature of Fairy Tales* (Indiana University Press, Bloomington and London, 1976)

Pantheon Fairy Tale and Folklore Library, Bloomington and London *Folktales of the World* Series (Routledge & Kegan Paul, London)

Ritual

Frazer, Sir James George *The Golden Bough* (Macmillan, London, 1936)

Gluckman, M. *Essays on the Ritual of Social Relations* (Manchester University Press, Manchester, 1962)

McNeill, F. *The Silver Bough* (Routledge, Glasgow 1957)

Van Gennep, A. *The Rites of Passage* (Routledge, Boston and London, 1960)

5 THE PHYSICAL ROOTS OF MOVEMENT: PREPARING THE BODY FOR ACTION

David Stebbing

These physical roots of movement are essentially as much about enjoying yourself and your body as about loosening up stiff joints and unrelaxed muscles. If you feel OK, fit and relaxed already, then you will find these qualities enhanced; and if you are also proficient at some sport or game then these too may be improved. This is because joint mobility and muscle flexibility are the root of all physical movements; improve these and you improve any activity in which you engage.

Life as we know it is expressed, experienced and also enjoyed through the movement of our bodies. The expression of ourselves, the experience of our world and life, are connected to physical movement, and our mental and emotional activities are bound up and inseparable from our physical freedom. In any body system, full function is the measurement of full health; however, the joints of most people are restricted, even those of many athletes and sportsmen, although rarely are they aware of how much. In fact this partial stiffness has become so much an accepted 'norm' in our civilised culture as to be of epidemic proportions and yet, as such, remains unnoticed. In the medical and therapeutic professions this is also seen as 'normal' when in reality it is often only a poor average and again it is then generally overlooked or ignored. As such this 'normal-average' situation is only partial living and partial freedom; a functional quality and natural sense of body enjoyment are partially lost and our personal potential is lying dormant.

This work is a concept originating out of using the weight of one part of the body and the gentle force of gravity specifically to lengthen and stretch another part through a process of active relaxation – a simple technique to improve body potential. This articulate stretching is also about discovering and exploring the roots and origins of movement, and thus at the same time it imparts an invaluable sense of body awareness. Basically, the powers, our muscles, move the supporting skeletal framework, our bones, at the centres of articulation, our joints – the focal centres where these forces interact and movement takes place. As the pivotal centres of all movement that we make, our joints are also the fulcrum of the way we express how we feel by the way we hold ourselves — as it were psychosomatic junctions. These junctions may get jammed up with the cross-traffic and residue of psychological and emotional stress and physical tension. So, stretching muscles and freeing joints may also be a voyage of discovery of feelings, limits and possibilities: the parts that feel good and the ones that do not — the supple, free-flowing, alive areas associated with good feelings of energy, grace and ease; and the blocks, tensions, hang-ups and fears physically formed and remembered in our tissues as stiffness, resistance, rigidity and sometimes pain. As such, stretching can be used as a powerful tool to increase personal potential, self-ability and awareness, and with these comes a gain in self-confidence. In addition, movement and sensation are increased and relaxation is improved. Gradually, body balance becomes better, and general awareness, health and well-being are enhanced.

Functional stiffness is therefore a form of habitual tension and stress and a state of being perpetually unrelaxed. It is gradual suppression of the once spontaneous human personality into restricted movement and attitude and is a kind of disease in itself. Here the ability to adjust freely and to be fluid in the physiological sense has its psychological connections — symbolically and actually. The problem is that as patterns of stress and inflexibility become habitual, we accept them as natural. At this point this may be just as much a mental or emotional response to what is happening as a physical one. But either way we may pay a heavy price in terms of suppleness, grace and ease in our world. Over the years these patterns of body restriction subconsciously tend to reinforce themselves. Patterns of stiffness and emotional tension are locked into the tissues, themselves a physical memory of all the past unresolved, emotional and mental experiences and traumas. At this point a closed circuit may exist. As we perpetually hold ourselves in an unresolved attitude to life in some part of our bodies, then the sensible response from that area becomes dulled, insensible too. So, that stiffness is a form of dullness and as our bodies adjust to habitual restriction and limited articulation, we become physically inarticulate and insensitive. Our ability to adapt and deal with any small overload then becomes progressively limited, as does our appreciation or awareness of how this is happening. In this way we are and become a product of our past experiences. For restricted movement is itself symbolic of all these life processes in us, and may collectively define the personality and self-image of the individual — representative on the one hand of our inner fights and conflicts, and on the other of our ability to project ourselves outwards and to interact with our world.

Ordinary exercise normally concentrates on stamina and strength, which is fine in itself but often leaves much to be desired in dealing with these underlying patterns of tension and stress. In this field there is nothing to compare with the therapeutic active relaxation gained by stretching your muscles and freeing your joints for their own sake. Discovering the roots of movement is not just exercise in the normal sense of the word. The stretching exercises work by nature and design, individually for each person at his or her own particular level; exploring boundaries, sensing restrictions and integrating feelings that flow with freer movement, some of which may have been asleep or out of consciousness for years.

In this work the ideal anatomical function is the guide, and the root of each movement the source, so that you feel the root and direction of each movement and achieve what you can. In this way the positive is used to express the possible and the potential. It also makes available a freedom to approach each individual on the same basis. These are simple and functional concepts and ideas of movement, from which the needs of the individual can be adapted as necessary.

You may be old or young, extremely body conscious or not at all, fit or physically disabled, helping others or yourself. The approach is the same: to gain the freedom to be what you want to be by unlocking yourself from the varying states of restriction of the physical self.

There are obviously limits to the extent that some can become integrated or physically well balanced and that some can move at all. However, it is worth remembering that there is a 'Zen-like' relativity in operation here. To those with very limited capacity, a seemingly small improvement can mean a lot — for an inch of movement gained is an inch of greater freedom won — and a more expansive world to move into.

This is creative and self-educational body and exercise therapy. If we are a product of our past experiences, this is one way that we can begin to take responsibility for the production of our future experiences.

Practical Activities

The exercises are designed to improve your body as a whole through acting on its various parts. The idea is to relax and harmonise muscle groups rather than to increase muscle power, but it is often harder to learn to relax than to develop strength. All the movements should be performed slowly and smoothly; no force or strain should be used, for this is directly antagonistic to your purpose. These are not exercises in the normal sense of the word, for the idea is to turn strenuous movement into ease and agility. Sheer effort is just not called for and a gradual build-up is more beneficial than trying to force your way through. On the other hand, not taking yourself up to your own boundaries of movement, so that nothing is felt, is also missing the point – 'nothing ventured, nothing gained'. Ideally, be just at the safe side of your easy maximum movement in each position to start with. Feel stable and balanced and allow the weight of your body and the force of gravity to take over slowly and, as it does, feel directly the stretch sensation in the specified area.

The tools are your own body weight and momentum plus the force of gravity; with sometimes the help/weight of another person, or a wall or cushion for added support. Many of the exercises are great fun when done in pairs. This works really well in groups, especially large ones, as it gets a good energy interaction going and gravity is made to work on your side.

Feel your way into things and take it easy, especially the first few times. You may find some movements easy. To state the obvious, you literally have 'body ease' in these movements. In others you may come up against personal thresholds of unease, disease and pain. Allow gravity to take over and do the work. Do not 'push' yourself or someone else past their maximum or extend them before they are ready. The idea is to get body intelligence and awareness working for you, so respect the body. I have never had anyone hurt themselves using this approach. The key is to give in to the movement and let go – take it as it comes, and just let the muscles stretch a little. Try not to resist and just see how it feels afterwards – usually good! Ease begets ease. Allowing gravity and sensation to take over, even if you initially come up against some pain, means that you are dissolving the stiffness (and the pain with it), increasing movement and expanding boundaries. After each movement a feeling of ease may be felt and after a whole session a general feeling of lightness and energy. Repeating a movement, for example 'hamstrings' (page 45), will allow you to feel the immediate benefit as you can directly feel the relative ease achieved in the backs of your legs on the second attempt. Initially it may take a few sessions to acclimatise yourself to this sort of body-work, although each session should be fun and beneficial. If you've already done some yoga and are supple, then it should be easy for you to 'tune in'. Conversely, with stiffness and inflexibility you may initially 'feel your stiffness more' the first time or so around; this is usually the first sign of body awareness coming back to areas where previously there existed a dullness. With a little perseverance these feelings will turn to ease and, in time, to pleasure as your body moves literally into a different world.

But a few words on 'pain'. It is basically a warning or message that something is wrong and most of us wish not to incur it, or to get rid of it as soon as possible. It may be harmful or destructive, as for example when lifting a heavy load badly or burning your skin. Bluntly, this is *putting pain in* and afterwards you are left with the harmful effects in the tissues and the sensation and pain to accompany it. (This is INPUT – DESTRUCTIVE – NEGATIVE.) In these exercises, in some areas, the initial confrontation with resistance and tension may be felt as painful by some. This pain in a way is already there, although you may be avoiding it by restricting movement. But the pain is a good one, as the stretching releases the stiffness in which the pain is enveloped. This is pain travelling in the opposite direction: *on the way out*. Immediately you stop, the 'painful' sensation stops. Afterwards you feel good, lighter, easier. This is functionally beneficial. (It is OUTPUT – PRODUCTIVE – POSITIVE.)

On Breathing

There is not room here to be explicit, but simply to say 'breathe'. This may sound stupid; however, many people hold their breath when concentrating on something. This works against you and in fact incurs tension. If you find yourself doing this during these exercises (or at any time), make a conscious effort to breathe, slowly and deeply with ease. This type of breathing can be used generally to enhance the movements and your ability to focus attention, relax and let go.

Hints

These movements are laid out to provide for a variety of abilities wherever possible. So, for example, a standing stretch may be achieved sitting or lying down. Thus if you are disabled, have past injuries or are just limited by excessive stiffness, there is somewhere, hopefully, for you to start.

In What Order and How Many: You may just experiment with a variety of movements or, better still, start from the top and just do as many as you can in the time allotted. Then pick up where you left off in the next session. When you become acquainted with the movements your own intuitive sense will help you.

Group Activities: The same applies as above. If you intend to use these stretches with other activities, on their own, or during workshops, have a loose structure by all means but also be flexible and 'play it by ear'. You will also find that you can let the stretches do the work for you, so let the participants enjoy them. Again, familiarity breeds intuition.

Children: Most people enjoy the playfulness of exploring body movement – children more than anyone. Of course, it depends on the age group; however, generally speaking, more movements with less time spent in each should be done with children. You may find that the exercises will initiate all sorts of free-form energy and movements. This can and does happen in time with adults too, but in a less exuberant way.

Disabled/Handicapped: After getting the relevant medical consultation where applicable, please do not be afraid to get them out of their wheelchairs and constricting braces, etc. and on to mats on the floor. You will need helpers here, of course. If a person is unable to do some of the movements, then get him to help someone who can. This helps immensely to support feelings of value, self-worth, self-responsibility and achievement. You may initially encounter an unwillingness to move or do anything in this group, for it can mean a lot of effort for them. But you may find that by the end of one session this changes to your having to curb their over-enthusiasm as you look around at their changed, bright faces. So it is well worth the initial effort. Of course, as with older people or any less mobile group, they may need to be taken at a slower pace and rhythm. Possibly finish with a 5-minute on-the-back short meditation or rest period if that seems appropriate.

Clothes: The freer the better, e.g. track suits, shorts and tee-shirts, etc. and bare feet if possible.

Space: Anywhere with room to move can be adapted. A comfortable space is obviously best, with warmth and fresh air and a carpeted floor or some mats if possible. In a warm climate, outdoors in the open air makes a welcome change.

Timings: The suggestions here are a general guide. You may wish to vary them when you have become familiar and proficient with the exercises.

Partner Work: You may wish to feature this in group sessions. People of all ages and abilities particularly enjoy working in pairs and it benefits the energy of the group. Generally it is best to do the 'individual' exercises first.

(1) Tailor position — Groin and Inner Thigh

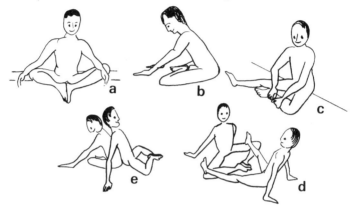

(a) Sit with your back against a wall, feet together and heels as close to your groin as possible. Place your hands on the floor and push your buttocks up to the wall so that the whole of your spine is supported. Gently work your knees towards the floor assisted by the weight of your arms. Feel this stretch in the upper thigh and groin. *Time*: 1-5 min.

(b) Forward bend. Flex and bend from your hip joints, and not from your upper back. *Time*: 1-5 min.

(c) With very limited movement. Support your spine against a wall and slowly bring your heel to your groin in easy stages. *Time*: 1-5 min.

(d) *Partner Work*. After doing (a)/(b). With your spine supported by your arms, take it in turns to place your legs across your partner's. Must be done slowly with care and with no sudden force. *Time*: 1-3 min.

(e) 'Back-to-back'. Slowly push your partner forward with your buttocks and lift yourself up into a back-arch over him. *Time*: 1-3 min.

(2) Squat — Calves

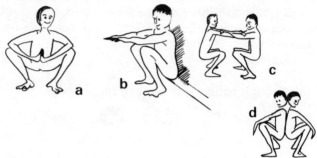

(a)   Start standing, feet slightly apart, and drop into a squat with your heels on the floor. Should be an easy position, with body weight forward and no strain in the back or shoulders. *Time*: 1-5 min.

(b)   This is easier. Slide down the wall into a squat position, or support your body weight by holding on to a heavy object, e.g. a heavy table. *Time*: 1-5 min.

(c)   *Partner Work*. This is also good if (a) is difficult. From standing, hold firmly on to each other's upper arms and slowly drop into a squat with your heels on the floor, supporting each other's weight. *Time*: 1-3 min.

(d)   'Back-to-back'. Start off standing and drop into squat position slowly as in (c). *Time*: 1-3 min.

(3) Knee and Ankle Joints

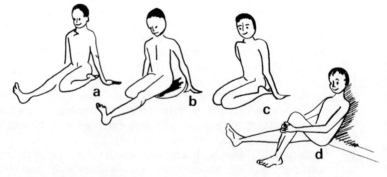

(a)   With your leg and foot curved around you, toes pointing inwards if possible. You may start off with the bent knee slightly out to the side if necessary. *Time*: 1-2½ min each side.

(b)   Easier position with cushion supporting the opposite hip. *Time*: 1-2½ min.

(c)   When (a) is easy you may attempt both legs together. *Time*: 1-5 min.

(d)   For very limited movement. With your spine supported, ease your foot towards your buttock until heel fully meets it. When this is possible, progress to (b). *Time*: 1-2½ min each side.

(4) Top Thigh Stretch

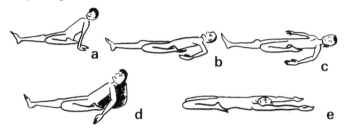

A continuation from (3). Feel the stretch in the powerful quadriceps muscles of the top thighs. Overtight quads often puts strain through the lower back.

(a-c) Lay back on to the floor progressively, base of your spine first, then lower back and then on upwards in that order. It is pointless to overarch your back to get further. Lightly squeeze your buttocks together to tip the front of your pelvis upwards and lengthen your lower back. *Time*: 1-3 min each side.

(d)   With stiff quadriceps, support your upper back with a pile of cushions and progressively discard them as the muscles ease.

(e)   If (c) is easy on both sides, attempt both legs together. Keep your knees more or less together. *Time*: 1-3 min.

(5) Inner Thighs

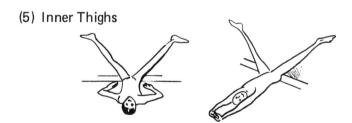

Lie on the floor on your side, knees bent, buttocks against a wall. Swing around, opening your legs out on to the wall into a 'V' as wide as possible. Use no force but allow gravity to take over. This stretches and relaxes your strong inner thigh muscles, the adductors, with your back supported and safe. *Time*: 2-5 min.

(6) Hip Joints and Pelvis — Primary Forward Bending

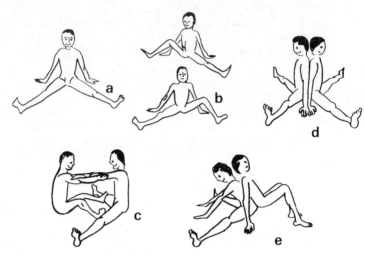

One of the main reasons for lower back problems is the loss of hip joint flexibility.

(a)   Legs fully apart with trunk straight. It is important to feel that you can flex forwards from your hips and not your waist, so, if need be, assist support with your hands and/or lean back until you can straighten your trunk fully. 'Lever' yourself forwards from your hips in this way, however small the apparent movement may initially be. *Time*: 2-5 min.

(b)   Bending each knee alternately helps to ease and feel this movement.

(c)   *Partner Work*. After (a) and (b), slowly and smoothly help your partner to flex forwards. *Time*: 1 min each.

(d)   'Back-to-back'. Push the bases of your spines together and support each other. Try rotating in opposite directions. *Time*: 1 min each.

(e)   Then, using your buttocks, slowly ease your partner forwards and lie in a back-arch over him. *Time*: 1 min each.

(7) Hamstrings

Many people are stiff and inflexible here, and many activities and sports actually tighten this important muscle group. This is also one of the first areas to stiffen up in children, so there are often years of tension stored here.

(a)   Feet hip-width apart. Flex forwards from your hips only, hands interlocked behind. Keep your trunk straight: it is then an efficient lever to stretch the backs of your legs. Then bend each leg alternately, keeping your back straight and body weight evenly displaced over both feet. *Time*: 1-2 min each side.

(b)   Same as for above, but more advanced. Feet hip-width apart but separated. Keep both legs straight, back heel firmly on the floor and trunk lengthened to aid balance. Feel this stretch in the back of your front leg. *Time*: 1-2 min each side.

(c-f) May also be done for ease or a change lying down or sitting, or especially with much stiffness or inflexibility. A thick cord or belt may help, as does the slight knee bending alternating with the straight leg position. *Time*: 1-2½ min each side or 2-5 min in all.

Partner Work. Not shown. May be done back-to-back as in (c-f).

(8) Calf Stretches

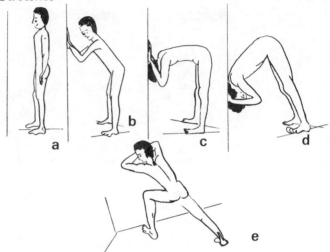

(a)   Stand 18-24in (45-60 cm) from a wall, feet hip-width apart.

(b)   Place your hands on the wall; start to let the wall support your weight.

(c)   Lean into the wall, getting the back of your neck and top of your shoulders on to it. Legs straight, heels on the floor.

(d)   Allow the wall to receive your full body weight, hands helping beside your head. If this is OK, slide slowly further down the wall, still with your legs straight. *Time*: 1-3 min.

(e)   Again using the wall, with it supporting your forearms and head. Back heel on the floor, front foot far enough forward to give you a good stretch in the back calf muscles. *Time*: 1-2 min each side.

(9) Neck

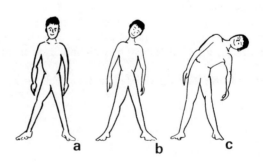

Feel this stretch through the side of your neck right the way down to your shoulder. A valuable movement, as a lot of tension builds up here. May be done *standing*, *kneeling* or *sitting*.

(a, b) From a vertical position, tip your head to one side, ear to shoulder, keeping your shoulders horizontal. Wait to feel the stretch in the top side of your neck: this means that you have relaxed your head. Then:

(c) Leading with your head, allow your body to arch over to one side. Stay about 1 min. Coming up is important. Do it by drawing up your top shoulder and letting your head follow. 'Sense' the stretched side in the vertical position before repeating on the other side.

(10) Pelvis — Standing Forward Bend

(a) Feet 3-4 ft (90-120 cm) apart and parallel to each other.

(b) Hands behind your back, lever your trunk forward, bending from your hip joints only. Try to keep your trunk straight and just 'hang' forward from your hips. This stretches the inner and back thigh muscles. *Time*: 1-3 min. (With ease and agility, stretch over to each leg alternately, and take your head to the floor still keeping your legs straight.)

(11) Side Stretch

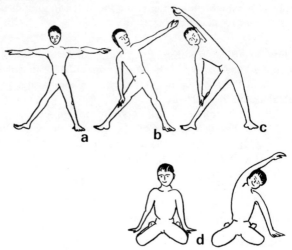

(a)   Feet 2-3 ft (60-90 cm) apart. This movement originates in the hips, so side-bend your pelvis away from you to facilitate free side bending and keep your body in a two-dimensional lateral plane.

(b)   Side-bend your trunk and support yourself on your thigh. Don't cramp your ribs underneath you.

(c)   Extend your other arm overhead, lengthening it outwards. Be careful not to curve your lower back. *Time*: 30 sec to 1½ min each side.

(d)   May be done kneeling or sitting. 'Support' hand at sitting level.

(12) Japanese Sitting Position

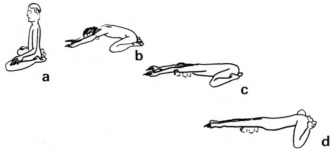

(a)   Sit between your heels, knees wide and feet curved in around you. If this is difficult, sit on your heels. *Time*: 2-5 min.

(b)   When this is comfortable, try levering your trunk forwards from your hips. *Time*: 2-5 min.

(c, d) Try to extend and lengthen your lower belly so as to keep your lower back from curving. Feel this stretch in the inner groin. *Time*: 2-5 min.

(13) Variations

(a)   Forward-bend to both sides from your hip joints and not your upper back or waist. Assist with your hands to lever yourself forwards, lifting up off the floor if necessary. Change around and repeat. *Time*: 30 sec each movement.

(b)   Lie forwards along the thigh of the front foot. *Time*: 1 min.
        (Not shown.) Lie backwards in line with the thigh of the back foot. Slowly progress backwards on to your hands, elbows, and on to the floor if possible. Only go as far as you can without overarching. Change around and repeat. *Time*: 1-2 min.

(14) Further Variations

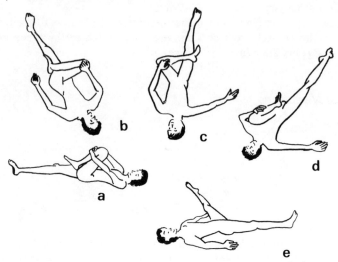

(a)   Knee to chest. Keep opposite leg straight on the floor.

(b)   With opposite hand, draw knee across body to floor.

(c)   Take bent knee back across, 'turning your foot over' as you do so and changing hands.

(d)   Stretch knee up and outwards at a diagonal. Keep opposite leg firmly on the floor.

(e)   Extend your leg straight out at a diagonal, other leg and hip firmly on the floor. Then slowly bring it around and down to meet the other leg on the floor. Repeat whole series on other side. *Time*: 1-3 min.

A good series of warm-up movements. Use a light, gentle, bounding movement and, as a guide, do it to a slow count of ten in each position. May be repeated a number of times. May be assisted for those with poor muscle control.

(15) Shoulders — General

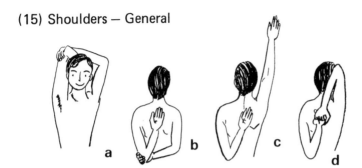

May be done *standing*, *kneeling* or *sitting*.

(a) With the arm overhead and back, pull the elbow into the mid-line. *Time*: about 30 sec each side.

(b) With one arm down and around your back, again stretch it into the mid-line.

(c) Lengthen the other arm upwards to the ceiling.

(d) Bring it back down to grasp the other hand. Hold each side. *Time*: 1-2½ min.

(16) Shoulders — Backward Extension

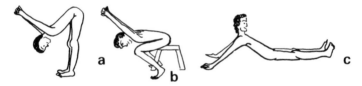

Variations of the same movement done *standing*, *sitting* or *lying* down.

(a) Forward-bend from standing, fingers interlocked behind your back, feet hip-width apart. Then extend your arms overhead and try to feel the weight of them 'hanging' over if you can.

(b) Sit on the edge of a chair, knees well apart if possible, Forward-bend and extend your arms overhead.

(c) Hands behind you, slowly slide them back trying to keep them from spreading outwards.
Feel all these stretches in the front of your shoulders. *Time*: 30-60 sec each.

(17) Shoulders — Forward Extension

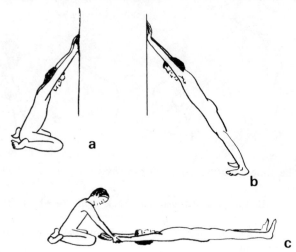

Variations of the same movement *kneeling*, *standing* and *lying* down.

(a)   Knees apart, hands as high up as possible on a wall, 'tail' tucked
       under. Lengthen your arms up the wall and just hang forwards.
       Time: 1-3 min.

(b)   Feet hip-width apart and about 2½ ft (76 cm) from the wall.
       Arms extended up on to the wall about shoulder-width apart.
       Let the wall support you as you hang forward from the top of
       your breast bone. Do not arch your lower back. *Time*: 30 sec to
       2 min.

(c)   *Partner Work*. 'Easy movement'. Your partner gently presses
       your arms to the floor, straightening your elbows at the same
       time. No force or sudden movement should be used. *Time*: 30-
       60 sec.

(18) Trunk Rotations

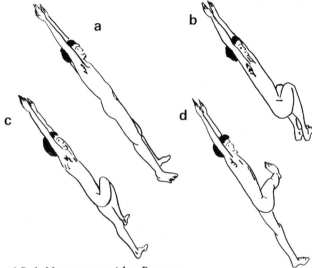

Easy and Safe Movements with a Partner

A natural continuation of 17(c). These exercises may also be done individually by gripping on to something solid.

(a)   Partner gently but firmly holds elbows and upper arm area down to the ground.

(b)   With both knees bent, slowly take them as far over to each side as possible.

(c)   Do the same with one leg bent and one leg straight.

(d)   If possible, straighten out the leg from position (c) and repeat on the opposite side.

All these movements should be done smoothly, with ease and in sequence, holding each position for about 15 sec. They may be repeated if enjoyable.

Rotation from Kneeling

May also be done sitting if necessary. As you slowly rotate trunk and head, it is important to lengthen upwards at the same time. Use your hands to support and assist you. *Time*: 15-30 sec each side.

Rotation with Two Partners

One partner takes the left (bent) knee smoothly towards the floor, the other gently holds the left shoulder down towards the floor too. This should be done passively and slowly, no force is necessary and it should feel pleasant. *Time*: 30-60 sec each side.

(19) Loin or Lower Back Stretch

(a)   Lying on your back, firmly bring your knees up to your chest, flattening and lengthening your lower back on to the floor. *Time*: 1-2 min.

(b)   *Partner Work*. On the floor as in (a), but with your arms overhead. Your partner carefully places his body weight to sit across your bent legs, just below your knees (knees may be slightly apart). This should feel really good and ease out your lower back, especially after back bends. *Time*: 1-2 min.

(20) Backwards Bending

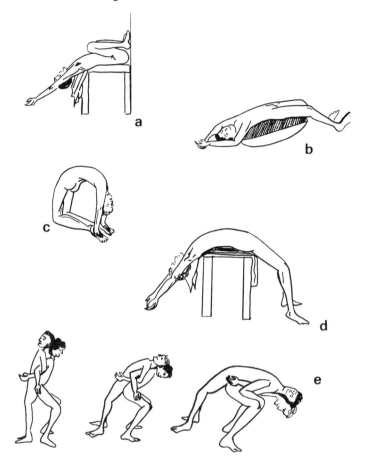

a

b

c

d

e

We spend much of our time bending forwards. Backwards bending acts as a purposeful antidote to this situation and promotes spinal flexibility and health. Feel all these stretches along the front of your trunk — belly, ribs, chest and throat.

(a)   Use a narrow table with a folded blanket to pad it. Lie over the table, feet on the wall. The idea is to keep your lower back flat. Let your head and neck hang freely over the edge. When comfortable, extend your arms overhead, keeping them straight. When you feel relaxed in this position you can inch yourself a little further over. The rule here is always to make sure you keep a little of your shoulder blades supported on the table. *Time*: 1-5 min.

(b)   Use a large, firm cushion, pile of cushions, padded low table, chest or solid box about 18 in (45 cm) off the ground. Let your head hang back and then take your arms overhead. The vital rule here is that your pelvis and shoulder blades are supported so that your spine is safely supported too. *Time*: 1-5 min.

(c)   Here you must start supporting the back bend yourself. Knees slightly apart, soles of feet upwards. Push your hips as far forwards as possible: this 'roots' and supports your spine. Take your arms overhead one at a time and grasp your heels, keep pushing forward with your hips and let your head drop back. Keep breathing, slowly but deeply. If there is any pain in your back during this exercise, stop and come up, you are probably not pushing your hips far enough forwards. *Time*: 15 sec to 1 min; may be repeated.

(d)   As in (b) but a fuller stretch using a higher, narrow table or bench. As in (a) you may inch your shoulders further over the edge. Be careful to make sure that the upper part of your pelvis and the lower part of your shoulder blades are supported at all times.

(e)   *Partner Work*. 'The backbend lift'. Fun if done properly. Ideally your partner should be roughly your own height and weight. Interlock your elbows underneath the partner you wish to lift. Then get your 'tail' well underneath your partner's buttocks, so that when you 'lift' they are well on to your back, with their 'tail' up into the small of your own back. Keep your knees bent and slightly 'turned out' at all times for strong and safe support.

Make sure that your partner relaxes into the back-bend and lets their body go 'floppy'. Most people love the sensation once they go 'floppy' and relax. When you place your partner back down, watch his heels between your legs and slowly place them back on the floor. Most people are delighted by this exercise and it can be a good one with which to end a session. *Time:* 30 sec to 3 min.

Spinal problems. 'Supported' back bends as in (a) and (b) may help. If these are OK, then you may try (c) and (d), if done properly and carefully. *These exercises should not cause back pain* so let that be your guideline and of course, if in any doubt, consult your doctor, osteopath or chiropractor.

(21) Neck

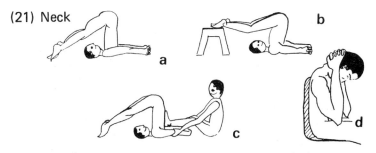

These exercises are good for the tension that often builds up under the back of the skull, which can set up headaches.

(a)   Lie on the floor, bend your knees up to your chest and, supporting yourself with your hands, take your feet over your head. Knees bent or straight, arms extended out in front of you with hands interlocked if possible, keep your head straight, with your body weight up on to the back of your neck and top edge of your shoulders as much as possible. Gradually ease yourself into this position and straighten your back. *Time*: 1-5 min.

(b)   Easier position. Place a stool or other support under your feet, but still aim to keep your spine straight. When this becomes easier in time, move towards (a). *Time*: 1-5 min.

(c)   *Partner Work.* After doing (a) or (b). Lightly grip your partner's forearms and gently, with bare feet, lengthen your partner's spine out, slowly straightening any bent or stiff areas. *Time*: 30-60 sec.

(d)   Easy neck stretch from a sitting position. With your fingers interlocked, bring your elbows close together and gently but firmly pull your head downwards. Do as often as you wish.

(22) Shoulder Work in Pairs

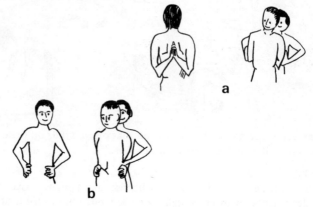

(a)   Place hands in prayer position behind your back and up as high
        as possible. Partner gently but firmly presses your elbows down-
        wards and inwards. Note position of helper's elbows for least
        effort and best effect. *Time*: 15-30 sec.

(b)   Hands on hips with care to place thumbs in front. Helper
        smoothly but firmly presses your elbows towards each other as
        you breathe out. Good to do gradually using three deep breaths,
        on each exhalation bringing the elbows a little closer. Should be
        enjoyable and fun. Have a go and relax into it, then swap over.

(23) Wrists and Forearms

Best done sitting on the floor. Start with your palms on the floor in
front of you, fingers facing forwards. Then rotate your hands outwards so that your fingers face back towards you, thumbs now on
the outside, palms still flat on the floor. Sit back between your heels
to get a good stretch through your forearm. If easy, start with your
hands slightly further away. If difficult, then repeat a few times.
Time: 30-45 sec.

(24) Hands

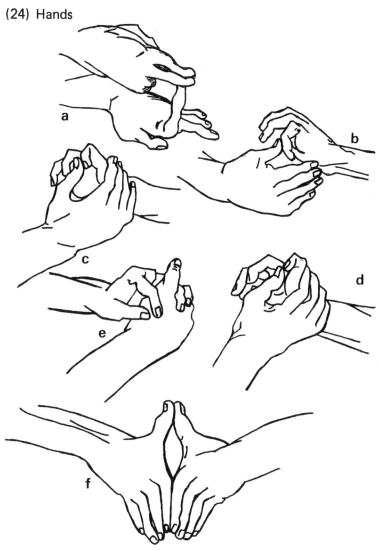

Our hands are superb organs of deft touch, strength and precision. It is possibly through the development of this manual dexterity that man has improved his mental capacities. The hands serve us well and we work them hard. Improving or regaining their full movement means that you are improving your capacity and ability at whatever you do. Just stretching your hands can often mentally relax and even revitalise you; as well as acting as an effective antidote to the work that stiffens these vital tools.

Do (23) first, then feel each one of the following as a positive stretch, held for 5-10 sec each.

(a)   With palms on a flat surface, extend or bend backwards each finger up to 90°, or a right angle.

(b)   Flex or forwards bend each knuckle in turn to its full movement by pressure on the first finger joint.

(c)   Flex each second finger joint in turn to its limit.

(d)   Flex each third finger joint to its limit by bringing the top third of each finger up to meet squarely the bottom third of each finger.

(e)   When it comes to the first or second fingers, the base of your thumb is more purposeful to flex these knuckles.

(f)   With palms flat on the front of your chest or abdomen, push your hands strongly together so as to separate quite positively the thumb and first finger.

Also (not shown):
Bend each thumb back towards the underneath of your wrist.
Using the whole of your other hand, stretch and separate each finger from its neighbour in a 'V' shape.
Rotate each finger and thumb both ways.
Finally give both hands a good shake out.

Good done any time on their own, as part of a workout or other therapeutic session, and a perfect way to end a session. Can be used for all ages and abilities and especially beneficial to those with already limited movement capacity and general body potential.

6 USING THE VISUAL ARTS TO EXPAND PERSONAL CREATIVITY

Roberta Nadeau

Because of the quite contemplative, personal approach needed in order to produce in the visual arts media, there are large expansive areas of inner exploration that go hand in hand. These inner experiences are of particular value to those who are using the arts with special populations. Most other art forms require another person in order to have a full encounter with what that particular art form can give. In the visual arts we can provide tools, knowledge of materials and experience with drawing and painting, which can allow individuals to take with them, wherever they go, the potential for further work. We have the wonderful opportunity to enrich their lives and creative potential.

Even in a crowd, the visual arts encourage a capacity to work in solitude. The artist's eye is always seeing, sensing and feeling the atmosphere around at that moment. If the inner peace for such exploration is not present in the person or persons we are working with in our initial contacts, we can at least see such peace of mind as part of our goal in introducing visual arts sessions. In this hectic, fast-paced world, all people can gain from knowing greater inner peace. Such peace comes from self-knowledge and an appreciation of each person's unique, individual, creative mark.

Theoretically there is a sweeping continuum. There are those working with populations who define themselves and their work totally within the psychiatric model. The work in the visual arts, at this theoretical point, is often interlinked with a psychiatrist or psychologist and has an important role to play in diagnosis and treatment. The theoretical continuum I am referring to extends from structured medical/psychiatric work to those working through their training in the arts and human sciences, and on to a far more experiential approach involving many of the people defined as 'special populations', each with the hope of expanding their opportunities and increasing their self-confidence and self-esteem.

The wonderful beauty of the arts, in all forms, is the fact of human emotion being involved in a raw and uncensored manner. Feelings flowing are essential for artistic experience. Freud, Jung, Plato and

Aristotle are but four of the thinkers who have as clearly defined the value of the arts in human growth and development. Freud helped us to be more aware of the unconscious mind and the necessity of the human being to have a full conscious as well as unconscious life. Dreams are essential to a healthy person. The professional artist and the inexperienced participant have in common the fact of being at their best as creators of visual imagery by their capacity to tap the unconscious and, as a result, to present in line, colour and form a mark that is individually their own, unable to be produced by any other individual in exactly the same way, ever.

The artist has always been a barometer of the health of a society. In addition, it is from the work of the artist that anthropologists, historians, archaeologists, etc. make the deductions so important to our present understanding of man's time on earth. Little of the written word has survived the centuries of human existence; actors die within their respected lifetimes; music survives and yet changes with each new person who sings the note, plays the manuscript. Yes, art changes too. However, sculpture, ceramics, and work in gold, silver and other metals have survived earthquake, fire, erosion and time. They have given to us from other centuries the visual information to conclude that certain instruments were used to make music, that certain types of theatre were important to the people of specific times, and that governments were organised in certain configurations. In essence, what we know of human history is a result of the work of the artist and artisans of particular times and cultures.

Despite often impossible barriers to creativity, the artist has been, through all time, a person of unquenchable thirst to know, see, feel and express through their work what they are experiencing. The art of any period of history is generally several decades ahead of actual social change: the pre-Russian-Revolution art and pre-French-Revolution art being only two examples. This response is the result of a phenomenon quite like having an extra sense. To the practising artist it can be a blessing as well as a burden, in that the capacity to respond to, record and assess the world around cannot be turned off. The artist does not work a nine-to-five day nor does an artist take a holiday. Art is a way of life, not a way to make a living. The creative mind is at work full-time, even in communication with the muses of artistic inspiration while sleeping.

I am here speaking of the creative process by which products of art are produced. All artists will testify to the fact that in producing one drawing or painting, ideas are therein born for another ten or more works. The finished product may at times be a great success or a great failure. It does not matter. What does matter is the continuation of discovery. This process is what we have to share with the people with whom we work. As Fred Gettins has said, 'Art is of value for the way it improves the mind and sensibilities more than for its end products.' Because of this exciting process and all-inclusive *seeing* and *feeling*, which are essential, it becomes easier to understand the enormous value of encouraging experience in the visual arts for those persons with special needs – the physically handicapped, mentally handicapped, elderly, psychiatrically ill, emotionally handicapped, socially handicapped and the economically deprived. Through teaching individuals to see what is around them, to express their feelings and constantly affirm the fact that they, and only they, can make those particular marks on paper or canvas, you increase opportunities for those people to know more about themselves and their unique rights for respect and self-love.

The use of line, form and colour are emotional encounters. There is even greater emotion involved once colour is introduced. It is important to know and to feel sure about the fact that art deals with human emotion, as quite often the act of putting line or colour on paper can produce cathartic emotional response on the part of the individual producing the work. Their excitement, tears and frustrations are to be dealt with sensitively – not in any way dismissed. For the very reason of such passion existing as an integral part of the art process, the arts have a vital role to play in allowing for increased quality of life experience for those with whom we are working.

Creativity is still a curious element of the human brain. Over centuries there have been attempts to understand, to clarify, and still here, in the 1980s, scholars admit that we know little about what creativity is. Yet readings and research confirm the fact that the creative mind is more in touch with self-discovery and self-development than the non-creative mind. In order for Sigmund Freud to develop his theories of dream interpretation, he knew that he had to begin with interpretations of his own dreams. Self-analysis also preceded his use of particular analytical techniques with the people who came to Dr Freud for help.

For persons who, because of unfortunate circumstances, have some form of disability, there are too often limited, if any, opportunities to realise the potential that exists within a body twisted, deaf, blind, paralysed or caught in terror. So simple is the procedure that it at times seems to me amazing that, for far too long, art materials have been seen by some as foreign, dirty (lots of cleaning up required), frightening ('we have no control') and misunderstood. Thus arts experience is denied to people who can gain so very much from it.

My heartfelt recommendation to those readers wishing to use the arts with special populations is to say, please *know* your art medium well. Know the unending desire to wake at three o'clock in the morning and return to a painting in progress. Know what it is to have cried the tears of joy as a work moves as you wish or, to your surprise, transforms itself into an experience far beyond your expectations. Know how to share that excitement, joy and frustration when things do not go as planned. For then, and only then, are you prepared to give honest and sincere inspiration to another person. Each individual will make his or her own individual statement in media best suited to his or her needs. Your role is to be a facilitator of knowledge in introducing the materials and to create an atmosphere where the creative energies of others can come forward.

Preface to Practical Activities

Art Materials

The art materials of concern to me in this writing are those that allow for two-dimensional expression; graphite, charcoal, conté, ink, pastels, paint, paper, pens, brushes, canvas and board. For a person who already has a limitation in physical or mental skills, it is essential not to create more barriers by improper selection of materials for arts expression. The materials should be of the best amateur artist's *quality* on the market place. Papers, canvas or boards must be of good size and quality. How destructive to say that you care to share the visual arts experience with a person of special needs and then to see only frustration because of easily torn paper, limp or lifeless colours, or 'self-destruct' creations, which are a pain to produce and a sorrow to the individual as their work is deposited in a waste can.

(1) Pencils (Graphite). Art pencils range from very hard leads to soft and very soft leads. For the purposes we are talking of here, purchase and use only HB, 2B, 4B or 6B pencils. Art pencils can be purchased from the HB end of the range to 10B; however, too soft a lead will defeat your purposes as the work created too easily smears. The importance of the soft leads is that it takes less physical pressure to produce a mark and even the most inhibited person will not find it difficult to deal with having once begun. We all are guilty of concluding that we

cannot do something and of being terrified to try. A simple, well-chosen pencil and a piece of large drawing paper can provide hours of exploration and accomplishment.

(2) Charcoal. Like graphite pencils, charcoal comes in varying weights or degrees of hard to soft. Again, purchase large sticks, which are easy to grasp, soft and, as a result, quick to make distinctive marks and absolutely excellent for the intense black areas that can be created. Charcoal does get messy and for some people that alone can be a most healthy and constructive experience because 'institutional' preference is for 'clean at all times'. For a person to be told, 'You have done nothing wrong, all will wash off when we are finished', is to be allowed to feel good, and is an affirmation of your belief in the individual's right to experience the joys of all levels of the tactile beauty and pleasure the creating of visual art allows.

Charcoal can also add new dimensions when an art gum eraser is employed to lift areas of black away. The 'positive space' imagery or design can be created through the efforts of working into a large black space. Positive space is the actual design area, negative space is the artistic term used for the space around the initial or essential design. For the mentally handicapped and emotionally disturbed this can be particularly gratifying, for they are creating an element of magic. I try to employ as much fantasy and magic-related conversation as is fitting in order to inspire and excite exploration.

(3) Conté. Conté is a stick resembling a unique blending of oil-pastel and charcoal. It, also, is available in a variety of soft to hard selections and in raw sienna and burnt umber (beautiful earth tones), black and white. Here, as before, purchase the softer, easier-to-use materials. The beauty of conté is the feel of silk in your fingers and the tremendous variation of marks, designs, lines and forms that can be made. The sticks, as with charcoal, have great versatility. A stick worked on its side gives wide sweeping flows of colour. The conté is easily smoothed or varied in intensity by the use of the fingers or a tissue rubbing the paper. Persons with limited muscle control can achieve delightful results because of the fluid capacities of the medium itself, and you will be happy to know that there is not as much washing up needed as is the case with charcoal.

(4) Pastels. These come in the form of chalk pastels or oil pastels. I use both in my work and recommend that both be a part of your art

supplies. Poor quality in choice will lead to two unfortunate problems: (a) the colours will be pale and bland, and (b) there will be great difficulty for some people to experience the goals you wish to achieve, in that the pigment simply will not move easily over the paper. One of the great beauties of pastel is that you are working with pure pigment, which has been rolled with a limited amount of oil to create a medium of pure colour. There are many varieties of good pastels for student or amateur work. Before puchasing, however, make certain that the colours are bright and the pigment is easily transferred to whatever surface would be worked upon. Even the most frightened or restrained individual can be moved to do preliminary explorations, purely by the excitement of the brilliant colours. The chalk pastels are soft and chalk-like in their feel in your hand. The oil pastels are more similar to crayon in feel, and yet are pastels, with all their wonderful qualities of colour intensity and capacity to be manipulated or mixed using fingers or tissues.

(5) Paint. Painting is a joyous experience which, as you will read later, must be introduced at the correct time to people so as to avoid frustrations and thus limitations to the gains that can come from the process. Again, your purchases must be made with concern for intensity of true colour and the manufacturer's quality of pigment transfer. I choose to buy tube watercolours, as so often the cake watercolours are difficult for many of those with whom I work to be able to know the full joy of flowing colour explode before them. I repeat: in working with people who already have imposed physical, mental or emotional difficulties, it is essential that we as facilitators for the arts do not put more barriers in their way by poor choices of materials. I never work with oil paints with groups. If a certain person wants to paint in oils, that becomes an individual decision between myself and the person involved. The turpentine needed as medium for moving the pigments in oil paints is very poisonous, and if an individual has allergic reactions to the turpentine, you have great problems on your hands. Acrylic paints are water-based, and water is used as the painting medium to vary thickness of paint and to clean brushes or hands. For many people interested in moving to thicker paints, I advise the purchase of acrylics.

Watercolours, especially from the tube, are most adaptable. You can teach a person or group how to obtain gradations in washes or to paint in wild, bright colours. To produce gradationed washes, you take a brush fully loaded with pigment. Strokes are made on the paper, and then, adding only water to the brush, a progressively lighter wash can be obtained. This provides, in work with the mentally handicapped or the senile elderly, opportunities to spark imagination with suggestions of a certain element of magic, which has become theirs with the use of the paints, the brush and water.

(6) Brushes. As mentioned before, buy good quality brushes. If cared for well, they will provide years of service to the artist's hand. I am not suggesting the purchase of sable brushes, but I hope to make it clear that a cheap 'bargain' will soon leave parts of the brush on a person's work. Efforts to remove a bristle can lead the way to the famous 'self-destruction' activity, which frustrates and can be heartbreaking. Also, brushes must be large - at least size 10 or larger — with adequate handles. There are some brushes produced by art supply companies which have a plain, unpainted and unvarnished handle. If you are able to purchase a variety of these brushes, you will see how their less slippery finish is a true blessing for certain individuals. The brush is a tool, an extension of the hand or foot of the person painting, and should be introduced as a tool. I will speak later of the importance of this understanding. As a tool, the brush can add variety to the experience with paint. It can provide unlimited variety in stroke, and in dabbing, pulling and swirling of colour. If you are unfamiliar with all a brush can do in your hands, I advise many lovely hours of exploration and fun before you introduce paint brushes to special populations. As with any element of knowledge or experience, we can only teach what we know.

(7) Inks. These come in many colours and can be applied with pen or brush. The use of inks as a medium of expression should be judged according to the people you are working with and their particular interests, capabilities and desires to express themselves in various media. Inks, rather like oil paints, take closer supervision or, at times, a one-to-one working relationship. Inks can produce great delight when used in mixed media works, and again, for certain individuals, much excitement when waterproof inks are used and then watercolour or pastel is painted 'magically' over the original line. For individuals with limited imagination, you as the facilitator may at times need to suggest media and approaches that can unlock some of the imagination which is simply lying dormant, since no one before has given it much of a chance. A point of interest to me is that here we must speak of all mankind, not simply those defined within 'special populations'. The opportunities provided to people all through life to explore their creative

potential are so very limited that they seem proof enough to me that we are tapping a most powerful source. If it were not so powerful, why should true creative experiences be denied to so many?

General Beginnings

Introduce one art medium at a time, and allow for full exploration and understanding of all the things one can do with a pencil, charcoal, pastel, etc.

Encourage an end to timidity by only providing large pieces of paper − paper at least 18 by 24 in (45 by 60 cm). Even the person with extreme limitations in movement will be able to feel the desire to extend their reach. In my experiences as facilitator of such extension of motor skills I have quite often seen attempts to reach the top and sides of the paper which have surprised the care professionals in charge of the particular individuals on a daily basis. Such extension was seen as unlikely if not impossible.

Some people can be assisted if you keep Velcro as part of your supplies, to wrap around the hand of someone who has little muscle extension in order to assist in holding a drawing medium or a paint brush. Also, putting mixed watercolours or tempera paint in empty liquid soap bottles (any plastic bottle that can easily be squeezed) may enable those with little fine motor control to enjoy all the glorious feelings of the painting experience.

Remain continually observant of persons in need of help or encouragement, but please constantly remind yourself that the beauty of the visual arts is the essential nature of *quiet inner discovery*. Constant interruptions or comment can break the inner peace of another person. We have been given as a right of birth the right to produce − we have not been given the right to disturb another's creative space. In my experience I have found that, presented with a quiet, mutually respectful atmosphere, the individual or group with whom you are working will wish to create an atmosphere respectful of all in the room. For some people, just to feel such mutual regard for their own thoughts, work and capacity to think can be as beneficial to them as the entire arts experience or their finished products.

Classical music, well chosen and played softly, can be a tremendous aid in producing an atmosphere conducive to creative activity. Here, however, I warn: know the music you choose and why it will work. If you are unsure or uncomfortable with the music, you can do harm rather than good. Bach's music for classical guitar and lute have been 'stand-bys' for me, in that they produce steady, quiet, soothing conditions of great musical beauty.

Provide a means of storage or transport so as to protect the creations of the people with whom you are working. Very few individuals have financial opportunities to purchase proper portfolios. However, these can be made by you and the persons in the group by saving any and all cardboard, sheets from packing cases, backs from drawing pads, etc. These simple materials and a little masking tape and time provide the person creating with a means of safe transport, and in some cases the only storage they personally can know, as this packaging protects their work while it is stored under their beds or in a closet in one particular type of institution or another. If you are able to have an actual arts or crafts room to work in, it is essential to provide storage for works finished or in progress. Some 'special populations' require that you find a way to lock their work away safely. Destruction or misuse of their completed works by another person, no matter how innocent or accidental the initial cause of such damage, may mean months of effort to re-establish the same quality of freedom in their artistic expression.

Have plenty of supplies and a large amount of paper. There is at times nothing so inhibiting to artistic creativity than to see limited supplies and thus, for example, to fear using the last remnant of a stick of red pastel. Having adequate supplies available has also, in my experience, produced a mutual regard and patience within a group. They know that even if they must wait a few minutes for the use of a certain material, it will not be gone.

Erasers should be viewed as tools and not as means of instant correction. Far more exciting results can be obtained by looking at other options of correction, such as darkening negative space or creating variations in shape and form which may not have been thought of if there were not a desire to change a form.

There is a great need for volunteer help if you are working with a group larger than three or four in number. Also I have had occasions where sisters, mothers, fathers, etc. have come along to a session to observe as they also provide transport. After numerous occasions on which comments were made, such as 'No, that isn't the way a tree looks', or 'No one has hair that colour', I decided that all volunteers or visitors would be given paper and encouraged to work. Suddenly, they too were having the same explorations and discoveries; soon negative and sometimes destructive comments stopped. Do remember that your volunteers are there to help you. Give them clear directions and encourage them to learn by doing what the artistic process involves. Otherwise they are more of a hindrance than a help.

Keep written records for yourself of your interactions with the various people with whom you work. These records are essential to your personal effectiveness as an arts facilitator/therapist and to your preparation in creating the proper time-and-space elements for each individual. The goal of one aiding others through the visual arts is to see positive change in self-esteem and self-expression, and an increase in motor skills and the quality of physical and emotional health of the persons with whom we work.

Be patient, very patient, if you have an individual who sits back only watching for a number of sessions. There have often been so many terrifying experiences piled one upon another to cause true and justified alarm when introduced to a new situation. Having created an atmosphere respectful of creative work, we then must learn to accept the flow of individual personalities. The rewards for such patience are great. An elected mute surprised all when she began to speak to me during an art session. She had sat watching for four sessions before participating. A severely handicapped young man made the first efforts ever to do things by himself and was so convinced that he had found his special way of successful expression that he asked if I could arrange a proper exhibition for his works. His family took him on holidays and he took all his completed creations in the makeshift portfolio I provided so as to show everyone. He had sat watching for five weeks before becoming involved. These are but two examples of the success that comes with patience and understanding. As certain people sit around the room watching, for sometimes even three to five sessions, when they, of their own will, approach you there is a rush of excitement and creative expression. For as they have watched, they have come to terms with the situation and have answered for themselves all the ever-so-important questions regarding how far to trust you as a person. Once the gift of trust has been exchanged, there is no end to the opportunities for creative self-expression.

Help yourself and others to get to know one another's names by starting each group art session with introductions. These exchanges of names can vary as the weeks of sessions move on. For example, members can give their name and then state their favourite colour or name of their favourite medium or image to draw or paint, etc. As will have been said by all the contributors to this book in one way or another, the recognition of a person's name and the time spent in helping others to know names can be very important. All that some individuals may have that they can truly call their own is their name. By recognising the importance of their name, you are recognising the value you place on their existence.

As many people in the populations we work with have been isolated from society, the sharing and showing of art history books can be a profitable period of time spent. There is a whole other world within the realm of the visual reproductions of other artists. Too many people have been exposed to nothing other than calendar art, television and a few, poorly done, entertainment-geared publications. Select the best and share the names of artists and the time in history in which they lived. Talk about what kind of painting you are looking at, or what the sculpture was carved from, etc. One or two pieces of work to share each session can be an amazing catalyst. If you are still working in pencil, charcoal and conté, show black and white drawings. Once working in colour, move into sharing reproductions of paintings. I had one young woman in a group of mentally handicapped people ask me very honestly one session, 'Roberta, could you help me make a Mona Lisa?' I responded with the gentle remark that it would help us both if one of us were a Leonardo da Vinci. That exchange led to many small discussions: never present too much to absorb at any time about Leonardo da Vinci. The purity of her keen interest was a true joy. Many an art history professor should be as lucky as I have been with students so enthusiastic and thirsty for knowledge.

It is essential in helping others create art that you have respect for the independent and unique mark they, and only they, can make. Even in the therapeutic setting, it is essential not to intrude, ask unneeded questions, or interrupt unethically the process of which we are privileged to be a part. If a person wishes to tell you about their work, you have received a double gift. You were initiator of the process and are included in the individual's enthusiasm and emotions about what they are producing or have produced.

One such exchange I shall cherish always. There was a severely multi-handicapped young man of 24 years who was in a group art session. He always arrived ready and eager to start. At this time the Falklands war was in full turmoil and he seemed to produce nothing but images of what he felt was going on. These images began to flow once we had worked together for a couple of months and he had all the media, except the paints, to choose from. One painting in pastel had a dark stormy sea, a dark troubled land, and a number of buildings. One of those buildings was a brilliant mix of pink, orange and yellow. The structure absolutely glowed from the paper. He asked 'Do you know why that building is there?' I had no idea. 'That building is where *the peace talks are going on*.' This exchange opened a door for us to discuss all his many weeks of battleships, tanks, etc. He had hoped that by drawing all these images he could get the war to stop. His words were, 'War is such a horrible waste of life.' Interference in his process of emotional release regarding the war, which was getting so much press and TV coverage, would have been unethical. Possibly such interruption might even have stopped his process of slowly creating adequate visual armies displayed on paper after paper until he was ready to create the peace talks within his gloriously coloured building. At that time there was, in the news media, only discussion of future peace talks. This young man was ahead of the politicians and more capable of producing honest images than some professional artists I know about.

Lastly, a most important element regarding the value of the arts experience upon which I could easily write an entire chapter: do encourage honest expression. Even if a person has ugly, angry feelings, which are finding their way to the work, you are succeeding, for these expressions are real. Work towards integrity and quality in the work of all people, and encourage truth of experience and sight. There is great damage done through allowing overly sentimental and stereotypical art to be produced by any individual. The value of involving anyone, particularly those defined within 'special populations', is lost if you passively allow the 'pretty' images. Because of lack of or limited exposure — and then at times only to the 'kit' art experiences, some people can easily arrive in your session knowing no other imagery than the sickly sweetness of the stereotyped art forms. By encouraging the reawakening of inner self and presenting activities that remove one immediately from such production, you can begin to encourage expressions of truth and personal satisfaction.

Practical activities

My attention in this section will be towards the use of the visual arts with a variety of people, with suggested activities which readers can adapt to their own particular theoretical frameworks or job descriptions. Personally, my professional approach is to offer actual experience within the visual arts and to know that the individuals involved will need to be attended to differently and responded to differently, and that the use of the arts in their lives must be individually defined.

I believe in the arts for all the various and glorious reasons described by myself and other contributors to this book. My intense personal conviction regarding the health of the arts experience for all people relates to the essential nature of the arts to provide for every person — man, woman, child, disabled or able-bodied — an avenue of personal expression. Only you can make that particular sound or line or movement. The other art forms dealt with in this volume sit more secure and removed from the tragic results of the trap I am presently concerned with. The visual arts have a hand-in-hand friendship with craft or, as I prefer to call it, the applied arts. The trap is that too many people administrating, giving economic support for arts programming, have in mind something very different from our purpose here.

Kits serve a merchandising purpose, not an artistic experience. Yet for so very many, 'arts programmes' kits are seen as the root of creative action. The final products are sold as commodities in giftshops. Often they are interesting to display, for, if the disabled individual has been able to move all threads as demanded, or paint pre-programmed proper colour in the proper space, you have a presentable but unstimulating and impersonal piece of work. These kits, green ware, paint-by-number sets, etc. do not allow an individual to express his or her feelings, to expand his or her capacity as a human being to feel, see or respond. As a result, such kits *must* be avoided at all times. The human mind is capable of tremendous creative ventures, which are all too frequently ignored or wasted because there are not enough people wishing to take the necessary time. Such kits also lead to the stereotypical reproduction of emotion. Our aim is to allow the people with whom we are working every opportunity to discover how wonderfully unique and special is the fact that they have known life and can share their feelings with us. To that aim, all our work should be directed.

Initial Experience, whether as a Group or as an Individual

People are often concerned and reluctant to participate fully when presented with a new experience. We must judge carefully what we introduce to an individual as a first visual arts experience. There are very few people who have not known, experienced, the use of the pencil. Even people I have known lacking arms have used a pencil from very early in their lives. A good graphite pencil, as I have described, should be used on large paper. Have everyone begin with drawing circles all over the paper, and, depending upon their individual abilities, encourage them to try to make the circles as similar in size as possible. The same should be done with ovals, lines and scribbles, the effort being to make the person comfortable with producing a line another person is seeing, and to break down all barriers to the famous saying 'I cannot do art.' These elemental forms are basic to most motor efforts used in writing. The fact that such simple efforts can bring true feelings of accomplishment are worth every minute spent. Every experience from there forward will reduce further and further an individual's inner fear. My own years of work with others has shown that there are people who will repeat, over and over again, the same imagery because they received such true pleasure from the first encounter. The circles or ovals will recur in works in pastel and paint – enhanced or matured through other experiences, yet a reminder of how important the first good feelings were.

Pencil

Circles, rectangles and scribbling all over the page. Tell the group: 'You can do nothing wrong. Art gives you freedom to express yourself as you wish.'

If I see a person being particularly withdrawn and afraid to begin, I ask them to hold the pencil or other drawing or painting medium. Then I slowly begin to move that person's hand (or foot). There will come a point where you can feel the person begin to take over the action. At that point I slowly release guidance and simply let my hand go for a ride. It will be obvious when you can lift your hand away and not have to give such assistance. For an individual with a limited range of muscle movement or motor control, this can be most important in assisting their efforts.

Charcoal and Conté

After a session or two with a pencil, I then introduce charcoal, a messy, breaking-free experience which renders on paper intense blacks and assorted variations thereof. Charcoal should be demonstrated as used in a direct drawing form; then with the stick on its side with the wonderful swirling effects that can be produced; smudging of the charcoal once laid upon paper; erasing – 'lifting' of charcoal with an art gum or charcoal eraser; encouraging people to feel the exciting fun of rubbing the charcoal on their fingers and then using their fingers as tools to create design elements. Hours of much pleasure to all can be spent. Simply make certain you have taken soap and towels.

Conté, although a different medium, can be used in much the same manner. The stick on its side can produce wonderful areas of variation. Into that area of pigment a person can again utilise the art gum eraser, or a tissue, to produce a variety of special effects. Actually, conté is more manipulative than charcoal.

Pastels

The chalk pastel is my personal choice as the medium through which I introduce people to colour. I have very specific reasons for this. When we as artists are working with special populations, there is great advantage in keeping, for as long as necessary, the pigment in contact with the fingers or toes. Not only are we, as people, more aware of the feeling of the medium against our skin, but we are also closer to the transfer of colour to paper, canvas or board. The intimacy of this process can be cathartic for some people experiencing the arts for the first time.

Colours can be layered, mixed, smudged or wiped away, leaving hints of pigment. All varieties of creative activity with colour teach fundamental understanding about colour and about mixing. The rich pigment of the chalk pastel allows for easy demonstrations and explorations of the *primary* colours: red, yellow and blue, and the *secondary* colours: violet, green and orange, which are derived from the mixing of the primary ones.

Each person responds differently on an emotional level to colour. The emotions and feelings evoked by certain colours are good to discuss. Small dramatic activities can be introduced where a person shows how a colour makes them feel — by the use of facial expression or body movement.

Oil Pastels

Oil pastels are easily over-layered, smudged, rubbed, etc. However, their particular qualities create unique results and experiences. For the individual clearly desiring to rub a drawing medium clear through the paper this can be of great benefit, in that layer upon layer of colour can be added and the product will only become richer — that is, as long as you have provided paper outside the 'self-destruct range'.

For a group of people working together over a number of sessions and who have been introduced to oil pastel, I have a 'trust game' (such jargon is a matter of personal definition, in that in the visual arts we are not dealing as directly with group activities as are those of our contemporaries working in music, the dramatic arts, or in guided fantasy through the avenues of folklore). This activity is to present to the group a large and sturdy piece of paper. The paper is passed one to the other as they individually work on their own creations. Each person should be given an adequate amount of time with the paper so as to make the contribution they wish. Their name should be signed on the bottom, with your help if necessary. Once everyone has added to the image of colour and form, the paper should be clipped to a drawing board. Then, gathering everyone around you, put turpentine on a rag and begin to rub the work. Turpentine acts upon oil pastel as upon oil paints; it is the medium of moving the pigment. Under a turpentine rag and with a little directed guidance on your part, a fascinating and beautiful group project can result. This is particularly pleasing to those persons with severe limitations to their muscle movements. Even the energy expended in one small corner of the paper by a severely incapacitated person has added equally to the overall beauty of the finished product. Such group projects I try to hang where they can serve as a reminder of group cohesion and of the elements of 'magic' that we, as facilitators/therapists, can put to our service. This activity usually leads to people wishing to experiment on their own drawings. I agree, as long as they will allow me to move the rag with their direction. 'Poison' is a word even the most severely limited individual understands. It is simple. You care enough for them to help them, but not to see anyone be ill or injured.

Oil pastel can also serve as a 'resist' for other media and greatly increases the opportunities for some people to experience the joys of the unexpected in the visual arts. When the person, or group, is ready to move on to experiences with paints, I first add oil pastels in mixed media work. I will speak more about this shortly. Once the individuals you are working with have experienced both chalk and oil pastels, it is advantageous to present both for exploration. As each medium responds differently to smudging, rubbing and intermixing, the results of beauty and fun can be delightful. Also you will soon be able to see how quickly certain people choose certain ways of working that provide them the most successful route to the goal they desire to reach, even if it appears to be not far removed from play to the observer. Picasso once said, 'To draw you must close your eyes and sing.' Working with certain persons within the range of our interests gives us increased insight into how much truth is in Picasso's understanding of the uniquely tactile, sensual and direct process of drawing.

Many works in pastel are known to us, through art history books, as paintings. Such a definition is largely the result of the paint-like quality of many pastel works. It is also related to the fact that pastels are such pure pigment. As I have said before, allowing the relationship between mind and hand to be as close as possible to the drawing or painting medium has many advantages for all who have a desire to experience colour. The emotions are more easily tapped because the paint-like flow of pigment on paper is so immediate.

Painting

I have already pointed out my particular desire for the use of tube watercolours. Egg cartons (of the plastic variety) or small cake tins can allow hours of unending enjoyment and exploration. I always begin by giving each person only the primary colours. By this time there has been an introduction to colour mixing during our time spent with pastels. However, a new experience results the moment you put a brush into the hand or toes of someone you are working with. The paint brush is a tool and it must be remembered that it can, for some, be a new barrier to creative activity. The brush allows new sensations and reduces the sensations of tactile immediacy with the medium. Assistance and patient, steady, guarded care must be taken, depending on the needs of the individuals with whom you are working.

I begin painting experiences by putting a bit of yellow, red and blue into spaced areas of the egg carton. We look at what happens when yellow is mixed with a bit of blue. The element of magic, or capacity to feel a power of control over a painting medium, can be, for some, the first experience with feelings of accomplishment and self-destination ever known. As I write I smile with delightful memories of the expressions on the faces of some people with whom I have worked and their incredible pride: 'I made *purple*! Look, it is purple.'

I help them see how the brush, loaded with pigment, gives a very intense colour, and how adding water alone to the brush will produce lighter and lighter washes. A bright red can become the faintest pink hue so simply, so pleasantly. One spring as the lilacs were in bloom and a group with which I had been working had begun explorations in paints, the demonstration of washes led one mentally handicapped young woman to produce the loveliest, softly whispered interpretation of spring blooms I think I have ever seen. She was not a master artist, with all the knowledge and understanding of the medium she was working with, yet emotion that flowed on to the paper made some of my professional colleagues' work look quite weak by comparison. She expressed the wonder of light colour, fresh new smells of the earth and the blossoms on the trees in a way I would be proud to approach in my own work.

There are many ways to use a brush: as a wash — the brush on its side, utilising the point to draw clear distinct lines, or by using the tip of the brush dotted straight down on the paper to produce spots, leaves, parts of a flower, a person's curly hair, etc. The brush, as a result, begins to offer extensions to creative process.

Slowly I add more colours from the tube watercolours to the palette of the people I am working with. Patience is truly a virtue in working in the visual arts, for if your excitement for a person to know more media or colours exceeds good judgement, you can end up with frustrated and sometimes frightened people — some who never return to the visual arts experience.

Also, do know that, depending upon the individual or the group, you may have to limit experiences with colour totally to pastel or coloured pencils. This may, for example, be necessary, as I have found, when the group you are working with is very large and your support staff is small or non-existent. Painting in such situations could lead to utter frustration for all, especially as there is a probability of water jars being knocked over or paints being confused. Spilt water is spilt water, granted, yet such spills can destroy the work of many and are not worth the risk. The objective of the arts facilitator/therapist is to provide creative experiences in self-exploration and it is of the greatest importance that we understand that we must consciously be aware of preventing situations which, by their nature, produce feelings of guilt or failure. If a person is angry with himself or his own work and purposely destroys what he has produced, we must accept that as his right. Group annihilation of all work within range of the running water of an over-turned jar is avoidable.

In working with the emotionally disturbed, we may often see outward destruction of the work produced. The anger is directed at their product and releases or responds to the emotions expressed in the process of creating the work. Conversation, one to one, about the work and your response can often provide insights important to the success of further creative activity with that particular person. Your own analysis of such behaviour depends entirely upon your training and your 'contract'.

Mixed Media

After all media have been introduced and dealt with individually, then and only then do I introduce mixed media investigations. After this point all arts media will be presented for a person's choice. The desire to experiment and to have fun is basic to human nature. There need be little direction given, simply your constant availability if there are problems, and your capacity to help and to encourage excitement in the people around you to try something new.

Collage

Collage work can be very rewarding for certain people, depending upon the restrictions they personally bring to an arts session. I save magazine photos for their beautiful array of colours and other assorted papers for their textures. Tear them up before presenting them if you are aware that people will only see the imagery and not the colours. Give a sturdy piece of paper or illustration board as a back surface and, with rubber cement from the jars, allow for imagery creation from torn shapes and areas of colour. To individuals with cerebral palsy, or those paralysed in other ways with limited use of their arms, this can be a most beneficial experience.

The frustration of struggling to have colour stay where one wants can be overcome with the assistance of yourself or a volunteer to wipe on the rubber cement for the people you are working with. Then as many variations of form or imagery as they desire can be explored. The fumes from rubber cement can be a problem for some people. Thus here, as in all cases, do know well the group or individual with whom you are working.

Rubber cement is pleasant to use for, once dry, the clear extra glue can simply be rubbed from the surface of the work. Some of the white non-toxic classroom glues can be used as well. However, they have one severe problem: many cause great wrinkling and here again a beautiful work becomes a sad completed work as it turns into a relief map. I imagine we have all tried the ubiquitous flour and water and we know of the discouraging crinkling and wrinkling of which I speak. Again I say, there have been many art and craft programmes offered to those 'less fortunate than we' and tragically all too often without a desire to see quality products result from the great rewards of a quality arts process. You simply cannot have one without the other. Because an individual may have a disability does not allow us, in programme planning, to offer second-class experiences. For the arts are too powerful, too important to human experience. They are possibly a major contribution to each person's chances of finding the appropriate mode of expression.

Working with Music

Some people are truly frightened to begin making marks on a piece of paper. They are afraid of judgement, of ridicule and exposure. I find that the introduction of music to the atmosphere of the session is most helpful. If you are going to use music, please know what music you are choosing and exactly what you expect to be the positive results of such a choice – as some music can be an unforgivable interruption to the creative process. Certain classical music, folk music and guitar can provide an avenue of personal transformation from a state of fear to one of actually flowing with the elements of the music itself. One mentally handicapped young woman I worked with asked, as a piece of Allan Stivell's Celtic harp music finished, who it was and how the name was spelt. I wrote the name on the blackboard for all to see, and she actually signed her particular finished pastel work 'Allan Stivell'.

Specialised Activities with Music. Certain music can be an excellent stimulus to creative activity, especially music well chosen by you to have certain rhythms, tempos and beats, which make automatic response to the music difficult, if not almost impossible. Even if the individual has extensive limitations to their personal movements, their minds can and do still respond. I generally put the music on after everyone has the particular art materials for that session. Then I ask for all to listen to the music for a little while and then to choose a particular medium that they wish to use, and to respond on paper as they would like to have what they see in their mind be understood by others. Slowly the efforts of all can be freed to a new level of experimentation and joy – especially if you take the time to choose music with variations which provide a creative stimulus, giving direction but allowing room for personal expression (see figure).

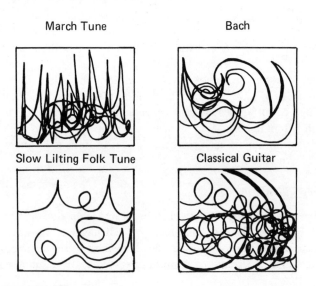

March Tune   Bach

Slow Lilting Folk Tune   Classical Guitar

A Partner 'Trust' Exercise Using the Visual Arts

If you have persons who are finding it difficult to get along, who possibly live in the same group home, work in the same sheltered workshop, or are in the same permanent care unit, then possibly via an arts experience exchange some of their feelings towards one another can be dissipated. In addition, it can help those concerned to understand better, or even to appreciate more their own capacity for patience. I must, however, add a warning: please know your group well and the two particular persons whom you involve in the activity, and expect no miracles. If you are unsure, change your own 'mind frame' to make sure you see this activity as a *game* and nothing more – a game to be experienced for the fun and artistic exploration.

We all feel rather possessive about our own work. It is natural and healthy. In fact, it is what I have spent the last number of pages writing about. If you have any questions about the following activity, work through it with a fellow artist or interested party before using it with a specialised group.

The specific activity consists of created pairs of people who will work together. One piece of paper is given, and conté, pencils, chalk and oil pastels are provided. The instructions are as follows. First, you, Billy, will begin. John is asked to watch and feel what might be the thoughts, colour desires and mood (these descriptive terms must be adjusted according to the group with which you are working). John watches silently and observantly. Then, at your discretion, you ask Billy to give the paper to John and for Billy to observe in the same concerned way. The paper goes back and forth several times, John and Billy making their own reinterpretation of their response to the imagery already on paper. The finished product should be hung in the arts session space or the exercise repeated at another time so that the participants can each have an agreed product as a possession.

I ask the reader to remember that some distances between individuals are there for reasons. At times unknown to us, cruelties have occurred that are too inhuman for us to deal with in creative arts sessions. We *must* be perceptive and never ask more of an individual than he or she can give at the particular moment. Also, we must understand and show compassion towards those in our sessions who have been hurt so deeply as to be unable to respond to another individual at all. Sometimes we can only know from behavioural signals, for which we must have our antennae out. We are not to be judges, only to recognise that, even among 'normal' people, executive, academic or working-class, cruelties may be imposed by a person which make respect for that individual impossible, in fact unethical. If we can understand this fact of life, why, then, do so many arts facilitators, therapists, social workers and psychologists feel that such problems do not affect those people who are described as disabled, handicapped, retarded, deaf, blind and so on? Human emotion is our common denominator. If one cannot hold total respect for individuals who do not want to work with those who have hurt them, then we had better go into another field where we are not dealing with the arts and with human beings and their emotional 'backpacks', which have collected survival equipment we shall never have the privilege to know.

A Group 'Trust' Exercise Using the Visual Arts

In this exercise activity, I always use music and involve the entire group. The activity begins with each person being given a large piece of paper. Then choices of the media are made. Once everyone is set and ready to produce, I explain the rules of the game.

(1) Names are put on the back of the paper and the paper is turned over. The drawing will now be placed on the surface facing you.
(2) Then each person is to work along with the music I put on the tape recorder *until* the music stops. Once the music is stopped, then each person passes the paper on which they are working to the person on their right. Each person again begins when the music starts. Music is stopped and the papers are passed again.

This continues until all the pieces of work have moved in a full circle. If Mary was the person you chose as a 'marks paper', then when that paper returns to her all members will again have their original work. It is important to select lively, steppy music. 'Stage show' music seems to work the best in creating an atmosphere of gaiety and fun. There will be some individuals who always watch their drawing as it moves around. I have even had people who are less than friendly say to another, 'Don't ruin my picture.' Even though there may be a few interpersonal problems, you should keep your eyes on the exercise as it is so very valuable as a shared activity, as an exercise in sharing. The success of the game will depend on your ability to allow people to know the great pleasure in all participants sharing and in being able to take home or back to their room a piece of work which has been produced by everyone in the arts session. I have done this many times with a wide variety of people with special needs and have seen nothing but pleasure and good will increase among members of the group.

Another Music and Drawing Game

In this game people are again placed in pairs. Each has his or her own piece of paper upon which they are working. If the person sitting facing another decides to add a form, colour or design to the other's work, they simply reach across and work on the other drawing. Again, lively, spirited music should be used, which creates a feeling of fun and party. There are very few times in which any negative behaviour has been exhibited. If you, as a facilitator, handle the games explanation well, it can be easily seen in the light of a game and as an experience most beneficial for all. However, some people need to be individually encouraged to touch the other's paper. We learn as human beings through such exchanges that new ideas often follow as a result of the inspiration given by another person's interpretation. Also, the opposite paper is always upside down to yours and the perspective is automatically changed as a result. The goal is to encourage trust and understanding through the exercise, which is structured in such a way as to encourage patience with another person reaching over and putting their mark upon your work. This effort to reach can be a physical extension activity as well.

One only has to be involved for a few minutes in any work to have a most personal identification which says, 'This is *my* drawing.' To relax with another person's intrusion upon our space has implications that go far beyond the art session itself. Goals such as these are a large part of the beauty of the arts as human exchange. We learn much about ourselves and other people, and the knowledge that we gain is essential for producing good art as well as for healthy relationships.

Creating Pictorial Images through Suggested Fantasy

For some individuals, if not a large majority of all people, there has been limited use of the imagination. We need, as arts facilitators, to have tricks up our sleeves in order to unlock creative thinking, or to remove blocks so long in place that it becomes a major part of our professional intention with certain persons.

One way I have found successful as well as most pleasurable for everyone is to select a fairy-tale or other richly written story in terms of visual imagery. Then, giving everyone paper and a selection of media, I begin reading the story with interest and excitement. As they listen to my reading they are to produce a work that expresses the way they pictured the story or the way they felt. Images, colours and emotions all are interpreted through each person's own perceptions. A well chosen story can unlock a great many of the blocks to creative thinking. The elderly person quite often finds great imagery provoked by stories that are historical-traditional in their nature. The great rich-ness that can be shared from having lived through so much of human history can be a beginning for awakening the creative spirit of a folk artist.

If the people with whom you are working have had little exposure to some of the great beauty of imagery-provoking stories, you should not panic as they sit wrapped in the story and unable to work. The images will flow later, and with such an obvious receptiveness for story-telling, you have an indication of the likelihood of success should the exercise be repeated.

Summary

In this chapter it has been my desire to provide an introduction to art materials and their use. I have included only a few of the many games and explorative exchanges that can be employed.

I purposely left out any of the psychologically oriented games or personal activities. My decision is related to my firm belief in the visual arts experience as a first-quality emotional experience for all people. I also have a concern for the specific intent of many such activities and the necessary psychological training that should accompany such work.

Also, I have not spent a lot of time in dealing with the art-related activities that are known so well by everyone, for example the glueing of macaroni in all shapes and forms to create designs, or of cracked eggshells on a surface to be painted. I know the reader can think of many more. Simply look in any elementary teacher's art directives and you have loads of such ideas. I am concerned with allowing emotional release and personal growth through the visual arts.

Your job is to provide good supplies, enthusiasm and creative inspiration. You will be needed as a keen and conscientious observer. Most difficulties can be overcome with a little help from you.

If you are fortunate enough to be working with a group of people in a situation where an exhibition of the works they each select as their own choice to represent them, can be organised, you have the oppor-tunity for a grand ending to what can be anything from weeks, months and sometimes years of working together. Such exhibitions should have a good accessible space and an 'opening' where others are invited and refreshments are served. This is a wonderful way to show people your appreciation for their efforts and to encourage further work and self-development through the visual arts experience. When such opportunities are not available, because of the conditions of a certain working situation, I have found that a finale can be accomplished through enjoying refreshments together. I give a present of pastels, paper, paints, or whatever would mean the most and be most needed. Then the highly emotional experience of having created art together does not end on a low note with simple goodbyes exchanged. You have been able to continue the inspiration.

I close with a reminder. We are working with other human beings through an emotional and highly expressive medium. We must always remain extremely *humble* in our interactions with others during working sessions. Openness to new experience is what we are encouraging and we too must remain open. So very much of what I have learned has been in response to what I have been taught by those whom I teach.

It is often thought that art is a form of recreation, indulged in by those who shun hardship. The true artist is never at rest, and such a giant as Rodin labours at his work with passionate devotion, from early morning until dark; indeed, after daylight fades, the dreaming muse begins to torment the mind until it can plunge again into manual expression.

The principles on which art is built are fundamentally the same as those of life itself. Sincerity of soul, accuracy of the outward and inward eye, constancy and patience are indispensable to any real accomplishment, be it art or merely living – perhaps the greatest art of all.

Malvina Hoffman
Yesterday is Tomorrow

Acknowledgements

For wisdom gained from working with other people I am forever grateful to Dr Dolores Armstrong and Dr Walter Hirsch. I thank them and all who, by their example, have given me such wonderful insights into the human spirit.

I thank Robert Whyte, Donna and John Harling, Sara Widness, and

Robert McInnis for always believing in me and my work; and all the artists, writers and poets of all time, for their unending inspiration.

Lastly I acknowledge with great love and devotion my husband, Bernie Warren — my friend, my lover and my partner in our work and intense love for others. I thank my children, Joe, Pat, Anthony and Noelle, for enriching my life and understanding of human existence, for always keeping my viewpoints fresh and clear and for returning to me so much love.

Suggested Reading

The following works have been selected as inspirations to creative thinking, artistic production and better understanding of the arts as a human process.

Arnheim, R. *Visual Thinking* (University of California Press, Berkeley and Los Angeles, 1969)
— *Art and Visual Perception — A Psychology of the Creative Eye* (University of California Press, Berkeley and Los Angeles, 1974)
Atack, S. *Art Activities for the Handicapped* (Souvenir Press, London, 1980)
Edwards, B. *Drawing on the Right Side of the Brain* (J.P. Tarcher, Los Angeles, 1979)
Feder, E. and Feder, B. *The Expressive Arts Therapies* (Prentice-Hall, NJ, 1981)
Kramer, E. *Art as Therapy with Children* (Schocken Books, New York, 1971)
Koestler, A. *The Act of Creation* (Hutchinson, London, 1976)
Langer, S. *Philosophy in a New Key* (Mentor, 1942)
— *Mind: an Essay on Human Feeling* (Johns Hopkins Press, Baltimore, 1967)
May, R. *The Courage to Create* (Bantam, London, 1979)
Pavey, D. *Art-based Games* (Methuen, London, 1979)
Stone, I. *Lust for Life* (Simon and Schuster, New York, 1934)
— *The Passions of the Mind* (Doubleday, New York, 1971)
Ulman, E. and Dachinge, P. *Art Therapy in Theory and Practice* (Schocken Books, New York, 1975)

7 DANCE: DEVELOPING SELF-IMAGE AND SELF-EXPRESSION THROUGH MOVEMENT

Bernie Warren

All living organisms, at least once in their lives, exhibit behaviours that could be referred to as dancing. Human beings are no exception. We are constantly pursuing movements that have repetition and rhythm and can be subdivided, by an outside observer, into movement themes or phrases. Many modern choreographers often build on these natural movement sequences to create aesthetic 'dance' pieces, which audiences pay money to watch.

Within all of us there is a dancer. Washing our faces, digging the garden or baking bread can all be viewed as our own personal pieces of choreography, our own special dance pieces. These movement sequences have special meaning for us and yet it is unlikely that most of us will ever 'perform' for another in hopes of reward, money or applause. However, they do reaffirm our being.

The movements we make as human beings are so intricately linked with dancing that many learned authorities spend hours debating when an action, or series of actions, ceases to be movement and starts to enter the realms of dance. This pedantic academic argument — concerning the physiology, mechanics and aesthetics of movement — is mainly irrelevant to the individual wishing to employ dance/movement[1] in a therapeutic setting. It is important, however, to realise that dance/movement pursues very important functions for all human beings.

For all of us the body is an instrument of expression and in childhood it is through the movement of our bodies that we start to build a picture of our world. As we develop we explore our capabilities and start to learn what our bodies can do. This exploration and movement of our body parts leads to a growing awareness of our body's structure and to the growth of body image. Not only is this early corporeal exploration important to the developing self-concept of young children, but also throughout life this testing and usage of our bodies would appear to be linked to cognitive development, particularly in the areas of assimilation and recall of new information.

More important still is the link between dance/movement and

emotion. The movements we initiate, the body shapes we form and the responses we present to external stimuli are indicative of our inner emotional state. The way we move, the way we stand, our gestures – all express more accurately than the words we speak what we feel at any given moment; in essence they express the 'sub-text' below our verbal communications. The belief in sub-textual communication through movement has created the concept of dance as a mirror of the soul.[2] This in turn has led to many referring to dance as the mother of all tongues because movement cuts across all language barriers and speaks to individuals at a primal, emotional level. For some people, particularly those born into highly technological and industrialised societies, which increasingly shun the expression of emotions, this can be *very* threatening. As a result emotional energy, instead of being naturally expressed, becomes pent up and is often dissipated through destructive or antisocial behaviour.

At perhaps its simplest level, a dance is a statement of emotion expressed through movement. To control the statement, to make it more specific, to produce colour and texture within the emotional statement, so that an observer (audience) responds, empathises or understands, requires a great deal of training, technique and 'emotional integrity'.[3] This is the arduous route undertaken by the professional dancer. However, as already mentioned, at any one time we all have at least one dance within us. Often those individuals with special needs, people who are disabled or emotionally disturbed, have a great need to allow their dance to see the light of day, for both physiological and emotional reasons. Yet all too often it is these individuals, who arguably have the greatest needs, who are denied the chance to explore this emotional release through dance/movement.

For the individual with special needs, the dance experience can be particularly valuable. For the person with a cerebral palsy, dance/movement can offer an opportunity to gain control over muscle spasms creatively. For the person who is withdrawn, a dance may allow them the opportunity to make a creative statement about themselves. For those of us making use of dance/movement in a therapeutic setting it is important to be aware of the positive benefits of dance/movement in terms of gross and fine motor control, neurological functioning, circulatory stimulation and so on. However, it is equally important to remember that the movements that form part of an individual's unique dance are an emotional response. It is this emotion which lifts the sequence of actions beyond the purely mechanical level of physical exercise, such as can be gained through racquetball or swimming. Dance allows an individual the chance to make a personal creative statement about their feelings through the movements they carry out. This will often have other benefits in more physiological areas, particularly for those people who have a physical handicap.

The implicit benefits that can be gained through dance/movement sessions are not easily achieved. For these benefits to be gained by individuals, it is important to engender a sense of fun and personal achievement throughout the sessions. If a sense of enjoyment and personal satisfaction is lost, the mechanical, physiological and neurological benefits that can ultimately occur as a result of dance/movement sessions will also be lost: as interest, motivation and self-satisfaction will give way to boredom, repetition and alienation from being just another trained dog jumping through the same old hoops.

The material that follows is not dance therapy or dance education in itself. Rather it is examples of exercises, games and ideas that I and other professionals have employed in our work with special client groups. The activities do *not* have some mystical power that can transform the neophyte into a dance therapist. However, the material is enjoyable, easy to use and normally 'successful' in the hands of individuals with little formal training in dance or dance therapy. Always remember that each group and each individual within a group has specific needs, and that sensitively choosing material suited to those needs will go a long way to making your sessions both enjoyable and successful.

Practical Activities

The material I present here is a cross-section of activities employed by professional dance/movement therapists. Some of the material is 'universal' and is also used by drama therapists, music therapists, etc. in their work. However, the roots of all the activities are in movement. The examples cover four of the basic goals a dance/movement therapist may be seeking to achieve with a particular client or group, namely: gaining greater control of isolated body parts; improving body image; achieving controlled emotional release; and becoming more socially adept. In many cases these goals are interlinked, for with greater control of individual body parts in turn comes a better appreciation of the body schema and therefore, an improved body image. This knowledge and control of the body and its extremities in turn facilitates the channelling and releasing of emotion through movement expression.

All the activities outlined require little in the way of practical equipment. For most, a selection of percussion instruments, or a tape recorder or record player to provide the suitable musical stimulus are all that is required. Certain activities may require specialised equipment and in these instances mention is made of this in the text. In addition, my own particular musical preferences for particular activities are also noted in the text.

As a final basic practical hint, I feel that dance/movement session participants should wear loose comfortable clothing, wherever and whenever possible. However, for some people, particularly in the first few sessions, wearing 'special' clothes can be very threatening and often counterproductive. However, in order that participants can achieve the greatest range of personal movement, it is important to work towards this simple goal.

Finally, try not to become so entrenched in the goals you are seeking to achieve for your group, and the individuals within it, that you stop being sensitive to a particular individual's immediate needs, or lose sight of the importance for all your group to become actively and enthusiastically involved in the session. Allowing the individuals in a group to enjoy the sessions, to have fun with you, goes a long way towards allowing the sessions to move from simply being labelled as therapy and actually starting to become therapeutic.

The dance/movement activities are presented here under four subheadings: Warm-up, Body Awareness, Group Awareness and Dances. It will become obvious to even the most inexperienced person that this way of categorising activities is purely a matter of convenience, as many of the activities outlined here could just as easily have been put under at least two of the other headings!

Warm-up

As with all other performing arts, a 'warm-up' period is an essential part of each session. The 'warm-up' is particularly important for people who rarely use their bodies, and well chosen warm-up activities will greatly reduce the chances of physical injury. Ideally, the warm-up should meet the needs both of the group and of the activities you intend to be part of the session. If the activities to follow are to be physically demanding, a thorough body warm-up is necessary to avoid sprains, strains or muscle tears. If the activities are to be more contemplative, emphasising sensitivity rather than activity, then a suitable warm-up is necessary.

There are many ways to warm up a group. If the reader should care to refer to the chapters by David Stebbing and Rob Watling he will find a number of excellent examples of warm-up activities. David gives a wide variety of activities that exercise specific muscles and joints. Rob gives examples of tag games, which are universally renowned as excellent whole body warm-ups.

Here are three simple warm-up activities. Unless otherwise stated, they are described from the point of view of the group leader.

Rob's Little Finger Game. This is an excellent preparation for tag games or a physically demanding session, although the title itself is perhaps a little misleading. I use this activity not only as a physical warm-up but also as a means of getting people to smile. In fact I treat them to a dose of 'humour of the unexpected'.[4] I tell the group we are to do a very strenuous activity and I ask if they think they are ready to do this. I then ask the group to stretch out their right hands. Then, after a brief pause to allow people to wonder what will happen next, I tell them to wiggle their thumbs. I always ask the group to be careful, not to strain themselves. After a short wiggle I tell the group to drop their right arms. As soon as they have their right arms by their sides, I ask them to stretch out their left hand and wiggle that thumb. I inform them of the importance of working both sides so as to balance out the body energy[5] — 'You might look lopsided if you only exercise one thumb.' Slowly I increase, without stopping, the parts of the body which are being moved, adding to the thumb: fingers, wrist, elbow, shoulder on one side, and then the other thumb, fingers, wrist, elbow, shoulder on the other side, finally adding the head, neck and hips until I get people moving all their body parts at the same time and hopping from one leg to the other around the room singing 'God Save the Queen' (or the appropriate national anthem). The effect is a chaotic mass of arms, legs, fingers and hips, counterpointing a rather august and nationalistic tune and almost invariably creates a light and humorous atmosphere.

This game is a good work-out for all of the body. It can also become quite physically demanding. Most importantly, it can be a very valuable diagnostic tool. It enables the leader to elicit information about the basic capabilities of the group early on. For example, does everyone in the group know where his knees are? Can everyone isolate a single movement such as moving his thumb? Can he* carry out more than one task at any one time? Does everyone listen to and understand control

---

*Please note that I have used the pronoun 'he' throughout this chapter to denote men or women. I have done this for reasons of simplifying linguistic style.

words? Do they laugh at your jokes? If an individual fails to carry out a command, there may be a number of reasons. For example, he may not understand the request. He may not associate the word 'thumb' with the relevant body part, or may be bored with the activity or deliberately disobeying – the possibilities are almost limitless.

It is important to remember that the warm-up gives the leader an insight into the likely capabilities of the group during the rest of the session. As a final note on this game, many years ago my colleague and good friend Rob Watling and I attended a conference where this game was played. The leader of the group (Tim) was a pianist who had a stump where his right hand should be, which led to an interesting adaptation of this game. Readers might wish to reflect on the simple changes they would have to make to adapt this game for people with limb loss or similar physical disabilities.

I am Me – a Name Game. This game can be played in two stages. In the first stage, the group stands in a large circle. In turns, each member of the group jumps in the air and as they land they say their name, for example 'Bernie'. This can slowly build until as soon as one person has landed the next person starts to jump, creating a 'jumping jack wall of sound'. This leads on to the next stage, where the group moves as individuals around the room observing the following ritual. The ritual consists of a linked pattern of movements and words, e.g.

Movement	–	Stomp	Stomp	Jump
		I	AM	SUSAN
Statements	–	I	FEEL	HAPPY
		I	WANT	ICE CREAM

so as to make a personal statement about themselves. This sequence is repeated until you feel the group has had enough. The first part of the triad is always 'I AM' but the second and third parts can be varied to I NEED, I HATE, I LOVE, I FEAR or whatever are the needs of your particular group. In each case the statements are linked to the movement, e.g.

Movement	–	Stomp	Stomp	Jump
		I	AM	JOHN
Statements	–	I	LOVE	SLEEPING
		I	HATE	WORK

and in each case the statements are always individual personal statements.

This game can be particularly valuable in enabling people to express vehemently their emotions without becoming 'spotlighted'[6] or having their problems focused on by the rest of the group, because their statements will be part of the group's 'wall of sound'.

Conversely, should you wish to bring the statements 'into the open' to be shared with the group, you can get the group back into a large circle and then ask each member of the group to cross the circle in the prescribed ritualised manner. As leader you can choose which emotions you wish each person to describe or this can be left up to members of the group. This can lead to group discussion or simply increase your store of information concerning the group.[7]

Follow my Dance. This is an adaptation of follow the leader using music. I always start the game with all group members sitting on chairs in a large circle.[8] It is important that each person has a good view of everyone else in the group and that they know one another's names. It might be valuable to play a name game immediately before starting 'Follow my Dance' just to jog a few memories. In the game there is a 'dance leader' who responds to the music playing. The rest of the group then tries to copy his actions. This leadership role is rotated among all the members of the group. The role is passed on by saying 'Let's all follow *Bob*'. So the whole group then watches and simultaneously tries to copy Bob's actions. In certain cases I take control and suggest that it is time to pass the leadership role on, or that an individual should lead the group for a little longer.

This is, for me, an extremely valuable and enjoyable game. In the past a lot of my work has been with groups whose movement capabilities were unknown to me. I used this game as a diagnostic tool.[9] Through careful movement observation[10] I was able to gain an insight into the abilities and attitudes of members of the group in a relatively short time and with little need to resort to clinical files or other sources of second-hand information.

An extremely important facet of this game is that it enables each and every member of the group to be 'spotlighted'. For a time everyone is the centre of attention and has power over the group. There is the safety mechanism that, should this be too threatening, as soon as the person starts to feel uncomfortable they can pass the leadership on to someone else. Also, when someone has been hogging the limelight for an overly long period of time, I, as leader, can ask them to pass on to someone else in the group. The length of time an individual wishes to lead the group is as important as the actions they do. It is interesting to note how the time individuals wish to spend as 'dance leader' changes, particularly in a group that meets regularly over a long period of time.

As leader it is important to start the group going. Remember that you must work slowly and in small stages. It is perhaps rash to over-generalise, but simple linear staccato movements, such as stretching right hand and arm out to full extension in slow small stages, tend to be easier for most groups to follow than large elliptical or circular move-ments, at least in the early stages. Groups can find sideways rhythmic patterns particularly difficult early on. This is perhaps a result of the 'mirror effect', i.e. instead of copying the actions, we tend, in the initial stages when facing a person, to mirror them.

I feel it is particularly important to be aware of individual efforts, especially when working with groups of people with physical disabili-ties. For one person, simply moving the limbs may be a great achieve-ment, and negative pressure to 'copy' the exact action may be extremely detrimental. In contrast, for others the inability to copy may simply be laziness or lack of commitment. These people obviously need coaxing. I always feel that when an individual is leading for the first time I should offer little or no direction during that period − I let them respond in their own way − for I need the first session to let me gain the insight into their capabilities before I can decide who needs help and what form this help should take: coaxing, pressure, stretching, etc. Having given myself this insight I can then choose music suitable to the group's needs for the next session. In addition, when I am leading, I can make my 'dance' include actions that stretch individual group members in the necessary way.

Finally, I always use music with a happy bounce during my first session of 'Follow my Dance'. The music is chosen to be specific to the age or ability of the group, but as examples I frequently use music by: Fleetwood Mac, Simon and Garfunkel, Mrs Mills (piano music) and Eric Clapton.

Body Awareness

Almost all movement requires at least a limited awareness of how the body works. To a certain degree, every movement exercise helps develop an awareness of how the body moves. The activities presented here not only emphasise body movement but also help focus on body image. In addition, many of these activities allow individuals to experience the link between body image, body movement and emotional response. These represent practically the soma/psyche linkage that dancers know all too well and leads to dance being referred to as '*emotion in motion*'.

In order that individuals may become aware of their full body potential, I feel it is important to help them feel comfortable with their surroundings, and gain greater awareness of the articulation of their body joints so as to enable them to start linking their kinesthetic actions to their internal emotions. For people unfamiliar with concepts relating to growth in individual awareness of surroundings and the movement of body joints, I strongly recommend the works of Veronica Sherborne and of Irmgard Bartenieff.

Electric Puppet[11]. I have various ways of introducing this game, depending on the age and ability of the group, perhaps the most common is the idea of the electric puppet. I split the group into pairs and then introduce the idea of the puppet. I tell them that in this particular case we will be dealing with a puppet that responds to a small electrical charge. I ask one member of each pair to be the lifeless puppet and the other to be the puppeteer. I then introduce the electric baton — a long thin garden cane[12] — which, in the hands of the skilled puppeteer, generates a small electric charge that is powerful enough to move individual parts of the inert puppet's body. I then demonstrate the workings of the puppet; for example, if the charge is applied to the right arm, it forces the arm quickly away from the charge and it returns slowly to its original position, and so on. I then ask the puppets to stand as still as possible with their arms relaxed by their sides. The puppeteers then go to work to see how efficiently their puppet responds to the electric charge. After a while I allow the pairs to change roles.

This, despite its dramatic framework, is in essence an exercise in body control. I always ask the puppets to close their eyes and concentrate on exactly where the electric charge touches their body, and then to move that part of the body quickly away from the charge, then smoothly and with the minmum of effort, as there is no more electricity left to power the muscles and thus the body part must work under 'gravity', back to its original position. This can be an extremely difficult exercise for some people. It is an exercise that requires a great deal of body awareness and control. Often the puppeteer starts with whole limbs — arms, legs — and moves to more specific areas — little finger, big toe — and more difficult directions. It soon becomes obvious to all involved that certain movements are impossible. Also, slowly the puppet learns to move away from the stimulus — often at the beginning people move towards it and I sometimes ask the puppeteer to leave the electric baton where it is *until* the puppet moves away from it.

This game can cause problems. As a leader it is important to be aware of people who like to 'poke' or tend to work at head level. With children, particularly those with emotional problems, it may be wise, at least at first, to limit the use of the baton to the torso, legs and arms. If the puppet is relaxed and focusing on the sensations of the body, it is not unusual both to sense the 'charge' prior to feeling it and to achieve a 'meditative' state.

Magic Aura. This is a good game to follow 'Stick in the Mud'.[13] I always try to find dramatic or imaginative frameworks to use with physical activities. This is partly owing to the influence of my work as a drama therapist and partly to my belief in the need to stimulate the imagination in order that the whole body can be totally involved.[14] This game is no exception.

I split the group into pairs. I then explain that on the word 'Zing' (or other suitable word; Abracadabra, Shazam, etc.) a magic spell will take hold of the group. The effect of the spell is that one member will become a frozen 'statue' but the other person will have the power to free their partner. However, the power will only work if the 'healer' works slowly and goes as close as they can to their partner's body *without* touching, but so they can feel the statue's body energy. If the 'healer' touches the frozen 'statue' he has to start again.

I always start the statues off in a standing star shape. This allows for a large area to be 'healed'. I ask the statues to close their eyes and both members of each pair to try to sense the body energy — to feel the aura. Once freed, the pairs reverse roles. Once both have explored the sensations and have been both 'statue' and 'healer', I ask them both to keep their eyes closed during the healing process. It is often during this part of the exercise that the healer can 'see' their partner's aura[15], even though their eyes are closed. If the pairs have a good rapport, the process can be repeated using more difficult and convoluted frozen shapes.

Again, this exercise can be particularly soothing. It requires a slow and sensitive approach by the healer and a relaxed but fixed posture of the statue. Children at first tend to want to rush through this game. In addition to the obvious benefits to be gained in terms of body schema, muscle control, etc., this is a valuable sensitivity exercise, with the selection of suitable pairs often being crucial to the quality of experience that individuals receive.

Ninja. The Ninja were a breed of warrior-assassins who were reputed to be able to perform such super-human feats as walking through walls, becoming invisible and breathing underwater. All of these feats were generated as a result of their extremely disciplined training, which emphasised mind-body co-ordination and control. This exercise is adapted from Ninja training exercises, and variants of the exercises are found in many martial arts systems.

Everyone is spread around the room with space to themselves. I inform them that the floor is made of rice paper and that great care must be taken if the rice paper is to remain intact. I then introduce the following stages one at a time, allowing the group to progress to the next stage only after mastering the basics of the previous one.

(1) *Point of 'absolute' balance*. Ankles shoulder-width apart so an imaginary line could be drawn from the centre of the heel to the centre of the armpit. Feet turned out 45°. Knees slightly bent, hips rotated to straighten spine. Back straight — imagine a straight line could be drawn from the centre of the Earth through the body up to the sun. Breathing in through nose and out through mouth. Weight can now be transferred easily in any direction *without* losing balance!

(2) *Forward walk*. Weight slowly transferred totally on to left leg, e.g. so that ball of right foot is last to leave floor. Right foot is placed back on floor so that weight is transferred from *heel* to *ball* to *toe* until the whole of the right foot is on the floor. The weight is then transferred totally on to the right foot as the left is removed. This process slowly gains fluidity until the walker moves forward without consciously having to think about the movement. If 'stop' or 'freeze' is called during any of these moving exercises, individuals should be on balance and able to return to 'absolute' balance with a minimum of effort. Throughout the exercise, emphasise fluid and light movements — no jerking or heavy moves or else the rice paper will be torn.

(3) *Backward walk*. This is the opposite of the forward walk. Weight is transferred to the left leg — the ball of the right foot is still the last to leave the floor *but* weight is transferred back to the right leg from *toe* to *ball* to *heel*.

(4) *Sideways walk*. This should be done as if you were walking with

your back to a wall casting a 4-inch shadow. It was mastery of the sideways walk, done in the shadow of a wall, which often created the Ninja's famed invisibility!

Transfer weight on to left leg. Replace right leg *heel* to *ball* to *toe*. Transfer weight to right leg. Lift left foot from floor, bring *behind* right leg and place back on floor *toe* to *ball* to *heel*. Fluidity is achieved by simultaneously shifting weight from right leg to left as left foot starts to 'grip' the floor.

(5) *Half-turn jump.* Jumping up and turning on the *'in'* breath and *'out'* on the return to the floor. A very small jump is all that is needed to create a complete turn. Often energy is wasted trying to jump high or through not linking movement to breath.

Throughout all the components of this exercise, participants can be asked to keep their eyes closed and to 'sense' where other people are in the room. Also, it is important to get participants to try to synchronise their breathing with their movements. This reduces the amount of energy expended in achieving fluidity of movement, leads to participants being more relaxed and creates a more meditative inner awareness of the body's movement. Many students, particularly those who have experience of Eastern religions and/or meditation techniques, describe this exercise as 'a moving meditation'.

In addition to the reflective aspects of the exercise, this is a great way for people to gain control over 'locomotive' muscles of the body. In addition to the control, I often add the 'release' of explosively exhaling the word 'kiai' on the jump turn, as participants touch the floor.

Group Awareness

Volley Balloon. The group sits in a circle on the floor[16] with participants sitting in a straddle position with their feet touching their neighbour's feet. A large balloon is introduced to the circle. The group has to keep the balloon aloft without losing contact with each other. Each time the balloon is touched, the score[17] is called, i.e. 1, 2, 3, until the balloon drops to the floor. You can introduce extra rules, for example, a person can only touch the balloon twice before someone else must touch it. In order to achieve a 'high' score the group must work co-operatively.

In this game the group is working physically towards a common goal while retaining a generally tolerable and unthreatening amount of physical contact. This is heightened if participants are encouraged to have bare feet.

The chanting of the group 'score' can become very ritualistic. This emphasises group cohesion and identity. Making the 'score' a competition, particularly against some 'unknown' other group, serves to emphasise this working together and group bonding.

Reed in the Wind. This is often referred to as a trust exercise; I prefer to think of it as an exercise in sensitivity.[18] One person (the reed) stands in the middle of a circle formed by the rest of the group with his eyes closed, his hands by his side and his ankles close together. The outer circle (the wind) place their hands gently on the reed. Slowly and smoothly they start to move the reed, who 'pivots' on his axis. Gradually the distance the reed is moved is increased from a few milli-metres to the diameter of the circle. In this exercise it is important to remain as silent as possible and the wind should always keep their hands in contact with the reed. After the reed has reached his maxi-mum point of travel, he is slowly returned to the central starting posi-tion. It is important always to begin slowly and not to fall into the trap of 'starting' from where the last reed left off. The 'laying on of hands'[19] – the point where the wind makes contact with the reed – is very important. Prior to any movement starting, and again after the reed's movement has stopped, there should be a time when there is a silent, non-verbal communication through the hands of the wind with the reed. The length of this communication should be dictated by the needs of the group – particularly those of the reed. At the start it is a time when the wind can reassure the reed, through touch, that they will look after him during the exercise. Occasionally the wind may want to hum a soothing tune quietly, for example a lullaby.

This is an exercise in which all the group are able to participate. Everyone who wants to should be allowed to be the reed. If a group member feels hesitant, he *should* be encouraged to try being the reed but he must always have the option to pass – without being made to feel guilty about it, either by the group or the leader! In many cases the simple 'laying on of hands' is as valuable, if not more valuable, than the gentle swaying motion.

Change. This is adapted from a Marion Chase exercise. The game is based on group cohesion and following a leader as exactly as the group's capabilities allow. (Obviously, when working with a group whose individual physical handicaps are diverse, allowances *must* be made to acknowledge the fact that certain movements may be impossible for particular individuals.)

The group stands, or sits, in a circle. I tell the group that I will do a repetitious action(s), which the group has to copy exactly. When I think everyone is synchronised, I will call 'change'. At this point the person on my left will be the new leader. Each time there is a new leader he must subtly change the action(s) and then repeat it (them) until the group is following exactly, and then call 'change'. In this way the leadership passes around the circle. This game can be seen as a further adaptation of 'Follow my Dance'.

I usually start this game without music and when the group has got the idea I then add music. The music that can be used is extremely varied; almost any LP or variety selection will do. I often use a tape that contains music by Eric Clapton, The Beatles, Henry Mancini, Allan Stivell, Joni Mitchell, Bob Marley and many others — in fact, a real 'Heinz 57'.

Once again this game allows individuals to be spotlighted and works towards emphasising group identity. The group 'dances' created in this way are often every bit as fascinating as some of the tightest show choreography and nowhere near as expensive.

Dancing

An individual's response to an internal and/or external stimulus is extremely personal. Often there is little structure that can be imposed, for there are no easily stated rules as there are with the dance/movement games. All that creates the urge to dance is the stimulus.[20] It is very important to have a wide range of stimuli available. What I present below are a few simple ideas.

Dance in/Dance out

I often use this with a group with whom I am working over long periods of time. It allows me a chance to see what the general mood of the group is before and after the session. All I do is play a selection of music before and afterwards and allow the group to respond to it in any way the music 'takes' them. Sometimes I ask them what sort of music they would like to hear — it is very important to have a wide variety of music with you — and as they will normally have a good idea of my selection, I can normally meet their requests immediately. In later sessions I often ask the group to bring their own music selection with them.

Once again I use observation of this free-form movement activity to supplement the other information I have about group members. To me my job is often detective work, trying to piece together a three-dimensional jigsaw full of emotion, where many of the pieces are lost or unknown. I find that any activity that allows me to step back and just observe provides me with a wealth of information in a far shorter time than most of the more directive activities.[21] The therapeutic use of the arts is very much a 'slowly, slowly catchee monkey' affair.

Feather Dances

For a long time I was stumped. I kept being asked to do worshops with severely multiply handicapped youngsters and I felt much of my material to be unsuitable. Then my assistant, Jane Newhouse, introduced me to peacock and ostrich feathers. From that day on I have been using these feathers not just with severely handicapped children, where they often form the bridge to my other material, but with all groups.

For this activity I use one of three specific pieces of music: Allan Stivell's 'Renaissance of the Celtic Harp', Howard Davison's 'Music from the Thunder Tree' and the theme music to Paul Gallico's 'Snow Goose'. I ask the group to lie, or sit, comfortably with a peacock feather in their hand. In the case of multiply handicapped children I work one to one with an 'able-bodied' person cradling[22] and supporting them. When the music starts I ask the group to follow the 'eye' of the peacock's feather[23] as it moves to the music. The feather often appears to have a life of its own and will 'take' the person holding it dancing.

With groups of severely handicapped children I ask their supporter to work through stages. First the feather is moved so that the 'eye' catches the child's attention. This necessitates making very small and fluid movements. Once the child's attention has been caught, place the feather in the child's hand and manipulate the hand so that the feather moves. As the child becomes more aware that it is his body moving the feather, the manipulator slowly releases the grip on the hand until the feather is moving totally under the child's control. The children may drop the feather – if so, simply put it back in their hands.

Lastly, add a second feather, so that there is one in each hand. These three stages may be traversed quickly or may take an extremely long time and a lot of patience on the parts of the supporters and the leader.

The ostrich feather is less of an 'attention getter' but it has a textural quality which fascinates many. The combination of peacock and ostrich feathers allows an extension of movement: a small movement with the peacock feather creates a huge and fascinating effect for a severely restricted child, and a sensual experience. The group can be placed so they work in pairs or, in the case of more able groups, they can freely interact. One word of warning: always be on the lookout for children who try to eat the feathers. It not only damages the feathers but can also severely injure the child. Finally, be aware of the other materials that can extend small movements of physically restricted individuals. Experimenting with different types of cloth, string, ribbons and so on can often find the materials best suited to your group's needs.

Music, Photographs and Paintings

Music, photographs and paintings can all be used to create a mood or to generate a response. The choice of a particular painting for the specific needs of the group is important. Having shown the group a painting, you can allow them to create a dance from the emotions engendered by the image. This may require choice of suitable music or may be better suited by silence.[24]

Postscript

The activities and games I have discussed are presented very much as I would do them. I have deliberately avoided trying to 'adapt' them for your specific group, simply because each group's needs are very different, although in some cases I have made suggestions. Always try to allow space for 'discussion' because often many of the dance/movement activities will lead participants to a new awareness of their actions. They may well want to share this with others. This may simply mean 'sharing' their dance, i.e. presenting it to an 'audience', or it may involve vocalising feelings presented while dancing.

Once again, the activities presented here are not meant to be a substitute for professional training, in either dance technique or its therapeutic applications. However, for those of you unable, for one of many reasons, to gain a professional training at present, I hope that the material I have presented, along with the suggested films and books, will provide ideas and a framework in which to continue your work. Finally, always remember that you are working with other human beings, their emotions and their well-being, and not simply playing or performing.

Acknowledgements

I wish to thank the following professional colleagues, some of whom I am lucky enough to count as my friends, for their work and vision and for the influence they have had on my own work in this field: Veronica Sherborne, Keith Yon, Kedzie Penfield, Walli Meir, Steph Record, Veronica Lewis, Jane Newhouse, Helen Payne; and particularly Lesley Hutchison and Chris Thomson for their support during my time with LUDUS Dance Company and Sensei O'Tani who awakened me to the way of the circle.

Notes

1. Throughout this chapter I will refer to dance/movement specialist or therapist. The reader wishing to pursue the topic further may wish to refer to Lange's *The Nature of Dance*, Bartenieff's *Body Movement* or Hanna's *To Dance is Human*.

2. The concept of soul is used here in the sense of intangible essence which is part of all of us, rather than in the more usual religious sense. Readers further interested in this area may wish to read Bettelheim's *Freud and Man's Soul* or Koestler's *The Act of Creation*.

3. This is a concept that applies to all performers. 'Authorities' refer to it in many different ways – it can be thought of as commitment to the role, an engagement or linking of emotion to action, or simply a focusing of emotion. The diversity of explanations regarding this almost universally accepted concept may simply reflect the problems human beings have communicating (see Watzlawick's *The Language of Change* and Gordon's *Therapeutic Metaphor*.)

4. A colleague, an historian by training and sociologist by profession, once advised me to 'always expect the unexpected' – a useful rule of thumb for the creative arts therapist!

5. This form of tongue-in-cheek humour I sometimes elaborate upon so as to include a discussion of Ying/Yang and the way of the Tao.

6. This relates to my belief that all human beings need to be the centre of attention, to be 'spotlighted', for at least a short period of their waking day. It builds on a number of other earlier theories and is discussed earlier in the book.

7. The way that any exercise/game is used depends on a number of factors, most notably the experience and training of the leader and the contract between the leader and the group.

8. One of my rules is that the group must keep their bottoms in contact with their chairs. This makes everyone equal when working with a group, some of whom are in wheelchairs. It also means that groups who tend to dissipate their energies by 'running around the room' are forced to focus their energies through their upper torso. With some I do allow them the luxury of removing the chairs: this causes problems of 'watching' the leader; my usual route for this is to do a floor-based version of the game, which often ends up resembling a 'Graham' warm-up!

9. 'Diagnostic tool' is a term I use to describe any activity which, in addition to producing the explicit surface behaviours expressly desired as part of its structure, also produces an insight into the capabilities and/or feelings of the

group and therefore allows me to build a picture of the individual which supplements and quite often contradicts the existing second-hand clinical reports.

10. Movement observation and analysis are *essential* tools for the dance/movement therapist. There are a number of formal and informal methods of analysing movements. I give a very rudimentary example in Part 3 of this book. This is no more than a starting point for further information see North's *Personality Assessment through Movement* or Bartenieff's *Body Movement*.

11. I first came across this game being used as an actor-training exercise by Dek Leverton, who is director of Pauper's Carnival, a Physical Theatre Company in Wales. I have adapted this into its present form, which I use with many different groups.

12. I tend to use a stick with a circumference of slightly less than the size of a dime or an English halfpenny. At first it may be worth using larger sticks, particularly with groups who have poor muscle control or kinesthetic awareness.

13. See R. Watling in this book.

14. I am not arguing for individuals 'consciously' thinking during kinesthetic activities, as all too often this leads to cognitive blocking of feeling sensation. However, I do feel that in order for the mind to be engaged, switched on if you like, individuals must want to be involved. Often a suitable dramatic framework helps to do this.

15. There can be a number of explanations as to why the blind healers see their partner's aura. Some require a leap of faith, a belief in the existence of body energy fields. Other more pragmatic explanations rest on the concept of feeling body heat and creating a 'mind's-eye' heat-outlined picture of their partner.

16. With some groups I have participants seated on chairs. The rule is you must always have your bottom in contact with your chair. This is a good way to integrate people in wheelchairs into the group.

17. Number of times the balloon has been touched by the group, before it falls to the ground.

18. All too often I have seen group leaders allow exercises such as this become an excuse to 'scare' participants to see if they will trust the group to let them drop almost to the floor. I use this exercise to reaffirm the group and to accentuate its sensitivity, care and concern for its members.

19. This exercise, carried out with a sensitive group, can practically illustrate the power of faith healers who are reputed to be able to 'cure' simply by placing their hands on people. The sense of well-being and caring generated by a supportive and sensitive group is very powerful.

20. There are probably at least a few dancers who have thrown their hands up in horror at this statement. I know that many dance/movement therapists do use/teach 'technique' to their groups. For the well trained ex-professional dancer, allowing the group to learn those techniques is certainly an option open to you. For those people without this training I feel strongly that you should be extremely wary of teaching 'technique'. All too often in unskilled hands it is synonymous with training dogs to jump through hoops and as such bypasses the emotions.

21. As a cautionary note: I feel it is very important to beware the 'This obviously shows. . .' trap! Although certain behaviours may be indicative of a particular emotion or state of mind, a single observation is *not* sufficient to enable *anyone* to make a definite prognosis. Humans are extremely complicated beings, not easily willing to oblige linear cause-and-effect hypotheses!

22. Those unfamiliar with either the technique or the importance of cradling should read Veronica Sherborne's work.

23. Please note that some children and adults can be extremely disturbed by this. If so, use an ostrich's feather.

24. All too often music is assumed to be essential to dance.

Suggested Reading

Background to Dance and Dance/Movement Therapy

Bartenieff, I. *Body Movement – Coping with the Environment* (Gordon and Breach, NY, 1980)

Bernstein, P.L. (ed.) *Eight Theoretical Approaches in Dance-Movement Therapy* (Kendall/Hunt, Dubuque and Toronto, 1979)

Hanna, J.L. *To Dance is Human – a Theory of Non-verbal Communication* (University of Texas Press, Austin and London, 1979)

Lange, R. *The Nature of Dance – an Anthropological Perspective* (Macdonald and Evans, Plymouth, 1975)

Sherborne, V. 'Movement for Retarded and Disturbed Children' in S. Jennings (ed.), *Creative Therapy* (Pitman, London, 1975)

— 'The Significance of Movement Experiences in the Development of Mentally Handicapped Children' in G. Upton (ed.), *Physical and Creative Activities for the Mentally Handicapped* (Cambridge University Press, Cambridge, 1979)

North, M. *Personality Assessment through Movement* (Macdonald and Evans, London, 1972)

Ideas/Activities

Bernstein, P.L. *Theory and Methods in Dance-Movement Therapy*, 3rd edn (Kendall/Hunt, Dubuque and Toronto, 1981)

Thomson, C. and Warren, B. (eds) *The Thunder Tree* (LUDUS Dance Co., Lancaster, England, 1981)

Shreeves, R. *Children Dancing* (Ward Lock Educational, London, 1979)

Torbert, M. *Follow Me* (Prentice-Hall, NJ, 1980)

Films

Bernstein, P.L. 'To Move is to Be Alive: a Developmental Approach in Dance-Movement Therapy' (1975)

Sherborne, V. 'A Sense of Movement' (1976)

— 'Building Bridges' (1982)

8 EXPANDING HUMAN POTENTIAL THROUGH MUSIC

R. Keith Yon

I teach music both for itself and as a means towards social competence: the arts fill the space vacated by smell-touch. This direction came about as a result of being concerned for singers who could be competent projecting from the formality of a platform, yet in the 'give and take' of informal contact became tongue-tied. I found it difficult to go along with any form of training that allowed music to become a mask behind which individuals could retreat, sometimes never to re-emerge. I became concerned instead that individuals should explore their feelings through music, but only to the extent that they had techniques to express them, in the attempt to balance inner and outer life. Inhibition may be defined as lacking technique to express feelings; maladjustment, on the other hand, is lacking the physical means to contain and identify them.

My personal experience of feelings is like inner movement, self-understanding, continuously fluid. Words, on the other hand, seem like articulated sounds trying to make objective sense, first to myself, then for sharing. When the gap between 'fluidity' and articulation becomes too wide, a link is needed to transform containment into expression: a period of refreshment between self-assessment and managing social contact. Music, with its sounds faithfully reproducing both sustained and articulated movement, and its language, which uses the elements of words, i.e. feeling-vowel and articulating-consonant, is, rationally speaking, 'non-sense'. But, on the principle that animals sing, whereas humans may speak — speech being heightened singing — music provides an interim state allowing feelings to be revealed that may not be defined in words.

That it is possible to express without communicating is all too familiar in moments of maladjustment. Often the problem is being unable to accept the 'echo' or comeback to one's own expression, whether from an audience of many or of one, or from oneself, in sound or silence. The sensation of hearing oneself is reflection after the build-up of feelings released in sound, e.g. banging an instrument, etc. When the habit of self-response is not inherent, an individual, familiar only with the sensation of 'giving', possibly as a result of early experience of touch emphasising handling at the expense of caressing, may find it difficult to cope with the vulnerability of remaining exposed and receptive to possible comeback, after having expressed his feeling. To avoid this he might concentrate his energy before the expression in a sudden build-up of feelings, which, suddenly released in the violence of hitting, kicking or obscenity, removes his sense of responsibility after the act, not unlike the relief after banging one's head against a wall, or after inflicting pain to express affection. Music, because of its potential for free and structured sound, allows exercise of feelings being exposed gradually, at the same time involving oneself and others.

In a North London school in which racially opposed groups had no time or space for each other, I found that by placing the rival Greek and Turkish, or black and white, groups side by side, they avoided confrontation, and could acknowledge at least the presence of the others; and having been encouraged to sing or listen to chosen songs, interleaving the lines of one group with those of the other, they had to experience silences alternating with sounds. The silences were initially antagonistic, but, gradually affected by the music, could acquire a semblance of coexistence. The change in the children's normal spaces and sense of time produced a musical form more relevant to their needs.

Play with spaces, time and forms proved effective in other seemingly remedial situations, e.g. actors having to sing, musicians to speak, visual artists to move and dancers to make sounds. Over the years this has extended to communication therapy with second language casualties, mentally ill patients and prisoners, arriving at my present concerns, which involve exploring expressive alternatives with handicapped people. My work model is a matrix, one axis of which is a continuum from handicap to non-handicap, and the other from individual to group; the individual who cannot move within this matrix, in any sense, seems to me to be handicapped. Essentially my work involves expression — gradual rather than sudden, considered rather than reflex, but I have had to become more concerned for finding inner resources through music: increasing an individual's capacity for feeling to the extent that he is motivated to find, rather than be taught, his most effective means of expression. My role as reassurer, then catalyst, changes to reflector to help the individual evaluate his experiences.

Music is my discipline; but my subject, for the moment, is communication. Communication, in my experience, is fraught at the best of times, but being normal means being able to brave the hazards of making and sustaining contact, even contemplating failure, because of having expressive alternatives to alleviate any possible frustration. Making sense of words may prove difficult, but their sounds and supportive gestures provide me with alternative means for sustaining contact. These sounds and gestures, developed as music and dance, provide those people handicapped in speech with alternatives of expression. Alternatives of expression are integral to body structure: the body is a torsal chamber at the gut-centre of which stimulus is accommodated and feelings are generated, and through the outlets from which, i.e. the arms, neck, genitals and legs, feelings may be expressed in similar actions. References such as 'being centred' have physical foundation. A sense of centre in the gut places the arms, legs, genitals and throat in balanced and supplementary relationship to each other, conducive to spontaneity, like animals, which we basically are. Familiarity with this sense of centre is to be encouraged in those who may be described as functioning from higher and lower centres (e.g. very heavy in body with little feeling of lift, or so 'heady' as to be out of touch with reality), and as being limited in their expressive potential. Individuals who rely on the eyes for contact and expression, e.g. the partially hearing, individuals in wheelchairs, etc., are inclined to strain the upper body and stiffen the lower; excess tension at the throat produces harsh and unattractive sound, and stiff knees make for general discomfort. The enveloping vibration of music provides a sense of overall reassurance, and the pulse of music, probably more effectively than any other sensory means, gets immediate gut-reaction and sustains involvement in that crucial region.

Music leaves no record, which makes it unsatisfactory as the means for exercising self-involvement for those who need the security of handling or seeing what they are doing; but is ideal for those for whom having to manage only one sense at a time is enough. Music related to body movement and play with objects has proved effective for both these groups, particularly as an interim stage between self-involvement and human contact. Relationships presume 'give and take' and may need to be familiarised in stages beginning with only 'giving' or 'taking' with inanimate objects to finding a balance. An individual playing with the shapes and textures of inanimate objects, e.g. toys, may dictate the length, position and modes of involvement. This one-way activity may be allied to experiencing noise, and to body movement, e.g. curling up as a self-contained sphere listening only to itself, as the basis of self-involvement. An extension of this is playing with animate 'objects', e.g. pets. This activity still accentuates the 'give' but the individual may 'take' the animal's response as he is able to. Such a reciprocal experience may be paralleled with 'animating' noise, e.g. banging or shouting through exploring its potential for rhythm interval and texture; moving the body between enclosed and erect forms, exercising the senses singly and in combination, fluctuating between solo and group involvement.

Throughout, rather than emphasising the specifics of musical language or appreciation of musical form, I have concentrated on integrating a sense of form into the body by experience to find a 'grammar' common to the arts, as an aid towards managing the morass of stimuli in life: a sentence is a thing (noun) enlivened (verb); a tune is a string of sounds animated by rhythm. Familiarity with this process of 'animation' may help to enliven the individual for whom the symbols of life have become stuck, including that of oneself as a cypher. Coming to terms with oneself as an individual functioning within society may be helped by the experience of singing or playing in a group:

(1) the same thing at the same time: tune, organum;
(2) the same thing at different times: canon, counterpoint;
(3) different things at the same time: harmony; and
(4) different things at different times: ?

The form of a song or symphony is essentially a journey in which feelings are transformed. For many their source of transformation, awareness of possibilities, is restricted to television soap opera, which is limited both in the spaces of the imagination and length of involvement. Musical form, not limited by narrative, may take the imagination beyond its normal expectation and give the individual a greater satisfaction from having structured a period of time creatively. With my groups I try to induce a sense of extended form by means of the format of the sessions themselves, both (1) of the individual sessions, and (2) as stages within an extended programme.

(1) That the session is experienced as a journey or story is crucial: all cultural groups use stories to reaffirm themselves. A story is a central event, an overall build-up, climax and release, sustained on a succession of subsidiary events, each smaller versions of the larger. So the 'journey' through the session progresses by stages of build-ups, climaxes and releases, through which the leader, like the story-teller acting beyond his normal body and voice, attempts to sustain a sense of overall caring.

It is worth making regular weekly visits to 'map' an inmate's time in an institution. These may be invigorated into a 'landscape' by exploring time, space and forms; rhythm, tune and textures. This is particularly important in those atmospheres of deodorant and Muzak, which as noise, effectively deprive the individual of his two main means of self-identity; body odour and sound.

(2) The length of the programme must be agreed. Even if the group is unable to comprehend fully a time-span of eight or ten weeks, I still perform a ritual, from halfway through, of a weekly countdown, so that at the end they may not feel suddenly abandoned: the parting is prepared and mutual. Arts experience aiming to help accommodate pain should avoid inflicting it. The final session cannot be the climax of the programme, but a time to release myself gently from their environment.

A class of intelligent, physically handicapped teenagers, conscious of their social prowess and the regard of their unhandicapped peers, found my sessions 'mad', and in order to be able to undertake the session, which presumably they wanted to, had to ritualise *every* meeting by protesting against what I asked of them. Responsibility for their 'madness' being removed on to me allowed them, within the secret of their classroom playspace, to enjoy themselves and transcend their handicap with impressive ingenuity and individuality.

The parameters of our relationship have also to be recognised. As leaders we aim to set up within the classroom an ambience of acceptance, and to provide a microcosm of society for individuals to test their personal and social expressive skills. But, in response to particular situations, we may need to limit our parameters to those of therapy, providing only as much time and space as those with whom we are working might be able to manage. In extreme situations, as helpers, we may need to become barely more than their physical parameters; actual body contact will allow us to become interpreters of their containment or expression. Within any learning situation, fluidity between the roles of helper, therapist and leader allows the artist which is in all of us to be revealed: to contest confinements, of body, society or sanity.

Practical Activities

Why is music of such value to me that I feel others could similarly benefit? Simply, music lifts me: my feelings, thinking and spirit are extended beyond the strictures of ordinariness, paradoxically by taking me physically inwards to my body-centre. This is not mere escapism: self-absorption is as distinguishable from indulgence as self-centredness is from selfishness. Having a centre to 'hold on to' allows me to move between moods which are normally judged as opposites, e.g. happiness and sadness, the one to be hoped for and the other avoided. In view of the fact that feeling is the source of action, it cannot be so undervalued, especially for those who find it unmanageable. Rather, the body should exercise its means to accommodate all feelings with the ability for transcending those that prove unpleasant.

Immobility of body, mind, feelings or spirit would constitute handicap; but seeing that these aspects of an individual may be interrelated, the immobility, for example of body and mind, may be remedied, or at least alleviated through the potential of mobility in feelings or spirit. Physical, emotional, intellectual or spiritual preferences of musical experience evolve from personal need; I would like everybody to experience what happens to me in music: the spaciousness of Monteverdi, the self-statement of Bach, the form of Mozart, the sense of time transcended by Schumann, the vibrant silences of Webern, the jolt out of complacency by Stravinsky; and to confront, as in many modern compositions, the relationship between music and life: music or noise, animate or inanimate sound. But being evolved in response to satisfying personal neuroses, musical taste must, in the educational interests of allowing others to function as individuals, be questioned in favour of underlying principles, directly related to the fundamental concern of individuality. This concern is to function within the pace, spaces and forms of society, which may be directly allied to the elements of music: rhythm, tune and texture. An infant exploring forms in space and time builds imaginative resources: an elderly individual is a treasury of images, needing only forms, time and space to be realised.

How this works in practice is best demonstrated in the format of a typical teaching session of mine: (I) greeting, (II) body-exercise, (III) sound-play, and (IV) reflection.

The Notes at the end of the chapter are in the nature of commentary and aim to highlight places where either I have drawn on ideas from beyond the realm of music, or where it seems to me that my practice may have relevance to specialists in other arts.

(I) Greeting

The group, including myself, is seated in a circle[1] on the floor, if possible (some may need assistance[2]).

(1) Hello. A simple song to greet each member: 'Hello Sue, Hello

Hamish', etc. 'Hello', sung, allows the 'lo' to be suspended as long as is necessary to gain the nominee's attention, which is then confirmed by naming: 'Helloooooooooo – Jim!' The suspension of the sound may be enlivened by repeating the 'hello'.[3] When it is possible for the list of names to be sung without suspending the 'lo', e.g. on one breath, an overall intention is set up; but it is more musical and structurally beneficial to phrase the names in groups of three or four.[4] The group, by pointing to each person in turn being named, might gain in concentration and focus, particularly in the case of those with no sound.

(2) Absent. Having celebrated those who are present, it is sensitive to remember those absent:[5]

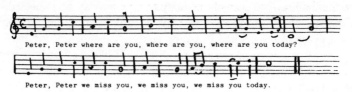

Peter, Peter where are you, where are you, where are you today?

Peter, Peter we miss you, we miss you, we miss you today.

(3) Framing. The group members, in turn, name themselves. So that each name may stand out individually, it needs to be framed, either in silence[6] or by the group repeating the syllables of the name, and clapping them,[7] e.g.

'Joe ✕ Helena ✕✕ ✕ Herman ✕ ✕ Dot ✕, etc.'

resulting in an exciting rhythm.

(4) Gestures. Each individual sings his name accompanied by hand or facial gestures, which are imitated by the group[8] either after or simultaneously with the singer.[9]

(5) Good Morning Signed. A more elaborate song accompanied by signing:[10]

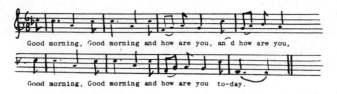

Good morning, Good morning and how are you, an'd how are you,

Good morning, Good morning and how are you to-day.

after which a contrasting coda is shouted, clapped and stamped:

Very well, thank you, OK.
the rhythm of a football chant.[11]

(6) Oh What a Beautiful Morning. This and similar popular songs[12] may be sung to get body and voice moving together, swaying from side to side:

'Oh what a beautiful morning; Oh what a beautiful day, I have a
LEFT –   RIGHT – LEFT –   RIGHT – LEFT –   RIGHT-LEFT –
beautiful fee-ling;   everything's   going my   way.'
RIGHT – LEFT –   RIGHT –   LEFT –   RIGHT.

(7) Events. Songs need sometimes to be improvised to cover exigencies, e.g. a birthday, a cold, a hurt finger, new glasses, an intrusion, a visitor, etc.[13]

Rudimentary musical experience is the difference between *duplet* pulses, i.e. two even beats, e.g. X X, and *triplet* pulses, i.e. two uneven pulses, e.g. long-short, X   X, or short-long, X   X; or three beats, e.g. X X X.[14]

(8) Rocking: Forwards and Backwards. This song accompanies forwards-backwards rocking, first in duplet and then in triplet pulse:[15]

Forward & back & forward & back & forward & back, stay for - ward;

pausing long enough to allow the body to curl into itself;[16]

back & forward & back & forward & back & forward & back,back,back,&c. ;

allowing the body to fall backwards and straighten out.[17]

(9) Rocking: Sideways[18,19]

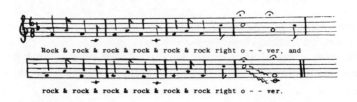

Rock & rock & rock & rock & rock & rock right o - - ver, and

rock & rock & rock & rock & rock & rock right o - - ver.

(10)Pull the Boat: Push the Boat. Modification of a favourite action song:[20]

Pull ♩pull ♩pull the boat   or   Push ♩push ♩push the boat gently down the stream.

(II) Body-exercise[21]

Individuals of limited or no vocal means need to experience song in their silent bodies: the musical lift through the feet, if standing, or the bottom, if seated.[22]

(1) Silent Song. Sing and dance a song, then dance the song: (a) without singing it outwardly, (b) without using the arms, then (c) without using the body or feet. Hear the song in silence.

(2) Humming. The group practises humming: 'Mmmmm', while curling themselves up; then, while stretching themselves out, they articulate the sound: 'Me-me-me', extending the vowel and possibly rising to the octave above.[23]

(3) Toe Song. This song accompanies massaging appropriate parts of the body.[24]

Oh there was a big toe,(big toe big toe)oh there was a big toe,(big toe, big toe)

oh there was a big toe,(big toe, big toe) and it reached up in the air

The last verse may be 'Oh there were ten fingers, etc.', in which case the word 'reached' may reach up the eight steps of the scale, with the hands trying to touch the sky and the body coming erect; then the cadence, instead of falling, remains open in a flourish of sound, after which the silent body tries to maintain the sense of flourish.[25]

(4) Body Blues[26]

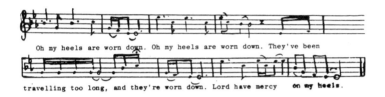

Oh my heels are worn down. Oh my heels are worn down. They've been

travelling too long, and they're worn down. Lord have mercy on my heels.

(5) Tarzan Song. A sequence of vocal sounds, duplicating those experienced slapping the body cavities:
'Foot///:Calf///:Knee///:Thigh///:Belly///:Chest///:Neck///:Mouth (Yodel).'
An alternative arrival at the top of the body is to roll the head around, humming in gentle triplet.[27]

(6) Rockets. Humming drones, as of 'engines' starting up, accompany hands massaging the thighs downwards to the knee, where they lift off; sounds duplicate their 'flight' to its apex, then sparkle, as 'fireworks', in a sustained cadenza, the hands, at length, returning to the knee-base and the voice to its drone.[28]

(7) Breath. Whether vocal or silent, individuals may exercise the three basic types of breathing: (a) breathe in and hold the breath till bursting; (b) breathe in and out regularly to counts, e.g. one in, one out, two in, two out, etc.; (c) breathe out for as long as possible.[29]

(8) Sentence. Build a song based on repeated parts of a sentence, e.g. (a) 'Today' . . .; (b) 'Today I am' . . .; (c) 'Today I am feeling' . . .; (d) 'Today I am feeling very tired' . . .; (e) 'Today I am feeling very tired because I got up late.'[30] Each phrase may be repeated until assimilated by the group, the breath between exaggerated with the lengthening phrases.[31]

Interlude

During the first part of the session the group should have experienced sounds ranging from very loud to very soft, indicating the parameters within which they may be expressive in the second part. The overall intention so far has been to treat the body as an instrument: as a group member 'tuning it up' first to contain feelings, through close body contact. Then for expression: individuals start to develop a secure physical base for creating sounds which allows them to venture beyond their bodily confines. An expression echoed by at least one other voice is the basis of communication; therefore, like an instrument, the body-voice has to be sympathetically 'toned' to respond effectively and appropriately.

An individual concerned only for expressing himself may be as way-ward as suits his purpose; but when intent upon communicating, be it with an audience of one or many, he has to accept the necessity for agreed structures, e.g. the conductor's beat, being in tune, being in step,[32] etc. This is how music is normally experienced and taught: the teacher presenting models based on accepted musical products within which individuals may choose to conform or rebel.

In contrast to this structured practice, music may be taught organi-cally, beginning with the crude materials of sounds which, through a process of exploration, become realised in individual forms. The dilemma of whether the finished production of a piece of music is more beneficial than the process undergone producing it, a topic which occupies so much pedagogic discussion, is in practice dispelled: process is product in a state of transformation, whereas product is process suspended. Whether structures or organic, the means for helping indivi-duals to create are only as effective as the leader employing them: ultimately I may communicate only the habit of conviction and moti-vation, i.e. what keeps me in one piece and what moves me to action: stillness and action. It is salutary to remember that an infant reveals in his rudimentary language an intuitive sense of symmetry: 'da-da', 'ma-ma', etc.[33] Musical form is simply the dynamic of knowing that a sound will be repeated, and being surprised when it is.

The relationship between process and product is crucial when working with handicapped people who, by definition, cannot manage the sharing of social 'products', i.e. cannot communicate, and who, to ensure that their frustration may be alleviated, need to be provided with alternatives, forms of expression evolved from individual rudi-mentary sounds. It is essential for handicapped people to experience something of the repertoire of music and songs to increase their sense of belonging in their society. These received forms, articulated intervals, structured rhythms, etc., which are the elements of 'proper' music, some handicapped persons may find difficult to accommodate, but through play they may in time assimilate them into their vocabulary.[34] It must be remembered that the musical sounds normally heard are articulated, i.e. played on keyed or fretted instruments, or are formal speech syllables: the gaps between, being sufficient to cause disquiet or excess tension, are likely to be abhorred by individuals lacking the technique for managing discomfort. Therefore it is essential to fortify the ability to accommodate stimuli by having the experience of more readily acceptable sounds, e.g. unbroken, melismatic intervals, which abound in folksong, jazz and Eastern music: a swanee whistle should be part of every therapist's equipment. Even more fundamental is the experience gained from playing with free sound, i.e. unstructured rhythms, microtonal intervals and noise: humming, grunts, expletives, banging, etc. It is not uncommon to find individuals, not only those who are handicapped, for whom the sensation of noise beating *at* their bodies, therefore requiring no response, is more to their liking than the spaces of rhythm and interval, which demand exposure of feelings. Transforming noise into music is finding the lifting quality of sound. Sound being an extension of the body must also be three-dimensional, and must reproduce the elements of the most immediate form of contact which it displaces: smell-touch.

(1) Depth. Animal sounds evolved to establish territory, clothing the body in vibration like an extra *texture* of skin: purring, humming, hardly more than an intenser layer of reassuring smell; by this means the body may choose either to isolate or express itself.

(2) Vertical. Changes in vibration produce notes of different intervals; *tune*, the change from one vibration to another, producing a feeling of suspension in the spaces between the intervals. Lack of interval, however microtonal, is noise.

(3) Lateral. Sound may travel where the body, for either physical or social reasons, may not: suspending itself in time, either sustained or kept lifted on articulating pulses, i.e. *rhythm*, which has the potential to behave with the dual characteristics of touch:

(a) as if handling, giving information, the one-way traffic of expression, favouring the control of duplet-pulses; and

(b) as if caressing, the two-way action of communication, sharing feelings, warmth oscillating in the space between bodies, favouring the expansive propensity of triplet-pulses.[35] The spaces between the pulses allow the body to be controlled or to soar; over-insistence on the pulse of rigidity of beat is tantamount to noise. (A lawnmower, moved by muscular effort, makes sound-phrases nearer to music than the mechanical rigidity of repeated beats from one driven by a motor.)[36]

Rhythmic patterns seem to be the property of the primitive and young, whereas sustained melody seems to satisfy maturer natures.

The following sections isolate the elements of music, in an order which is perhaps more accessible to handicapped people: rhythm, tune, texture. They attempt to provide: first, scope for both structured and organic processes of creativity, which is to say, forms as the bases rather than the ideals of exploration; secondly, rudiments for developing from accommodation to assimilation; and finally, group and individual involvement. Throughout, the essentials of creativity should be kept to the fore:

(a) listening – going into oneself: is it sound or silence?
(b) play – sorting things out: is it noise or music? and
(c) formalising – moving into expression or action: is it relevant, animated?

Where I have thought it helpful, I have related the elements of music to other media;[37] and because I firmly support the notion that instrumental sounds should be related to the body-voice, I shall continue to limit examples to the voice, hoping that their application to music generally is obvious.[38]

(III)Sound-play: (A) Rhythm

This section exercises the lateral aspect of music; breath or sound phrases conveyed over a period of time, either sustained (1 to 4) or articulated by pulses (5 to 11), allowing choice of being secure on the pulses or expansive between them.[39]

(1) Tennis. Pairs face each other throwing sounds across to each other, tracing the 'flight of the ball' with their hands and voices.[40]

(2) Ball of String. In a circle, individuals pass round a ball of string, humming and changing pitch as the string changes hands. When the string is substituted by sound being 'handed' around, the changing notes may be sung by the group, or individuals may hold on to their notes, building a block of sound. The changing notes may simply 'climb' the scale: 1 to 8 for the diatonic, and 1 to 5 for the pentatonic.

(3) Star Points. A piece of string is passed across the circle preferably of an odd number above five, to any but a neighbour. When the string is returned to its beginning the points of a star will have been created. If the group is numbered consecutively, the passage of the string, picked out on the numbered keys of, say, a xylophone, will make a

'star-tune' to which words may be added.[41]

The string is best passed through the spokes of chairs, allowing the 'star' to be placed near the floor providing 'hopscotch' spaces, each space a different note; then, if moved up and down the spokes, the flat, two-dimensional figure becomes three-dimensional, among the shapes of which individuals may crawl, tracing the lines of string in sustained and changing notes.[42]

(4) Star Radials. One end of a large ball of string is secured to the floor in the centre of the circle. Each group-member in turn is responsible for creating a radial, pointing in the direction he wishes his radial to go, and sustaining a note or gesture for the length he wishes the radial to be as the leader moves the string from centre until the sound terminates, i.e. the radial reaches its 'point'. The string is secured to the floor and returned to the centre for the next group member to create a radial.

(5) Support Music. The group sits in a semicircle,[43] and its members make sounds to accompany individuals in turn travelling to a spot that may be defined by a large card on the floor; different textures of sound may be explored to parallel the walking, which build in intensity as the traveller nears his goal. When he steps on to the card, the accompanying group sustains a sound for as long as he chooses to remain on it: then they accompany his return journey.[44]

(6) Tile-dance Chorus. Individuals choose a sequence of coloured floor tiles as a step pattern to be repeated as a dance chorus, e.g. 'Blue tile, blue tile, red tile, yellow; who is now a clever fellow?' Between the choruses individuals may improvise free steps and sounds.

(7) Stepping-stones. The 'banks of a river' are defined on the floor, and individuals, in actuality and in sound, try to cross in one go; the 'river' is widened until stepping-stones — large pieces of card — are required to facilitate crossing. Travellers, accompanied by group chorus, may either:

(a) linger on each 'stone' to admire or reflect on the 'landscape' of sounds, the quality of which is different on each 'stone';[45] or
(b) move across with urgency, which will result in regular steps and the syncopated lift taking precedence over the step.[46] On reaching the other 'bank', the traveller, accompanied by the group, releases the

tension built up in the crossing, in a cadenza of triumphant sound, particularly after the second mode of crossing.[47]

(8) Football Chant. Four cards are equally spaced in line on the floor; the leader maintains a regular pulse, singing and/or clicking fingers:

(a) the group, in single file, travel along the cards singing in time with the pulse, each beginning when the one before has completed the line, resulting in a continuous line of sound;

(b) another set of four cards is added:

```
|  |  |  |     |  |  |  |
X  X  X  X  /  X  X  X  X;
```

(c) card 3 of each set is halved:[48]

```
X  X  X  X  X  /  X  X  X  X  X;
```

(d) card 1 of set 2 is halved:

```
|  |  ⊓  |     ⊓  |  ⊓  |
X  X  X  X  X  /  X  X  X  X  X  X;
```

(e) the cards of set 2 are rearranged:

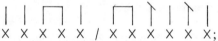

```
X  X  X  X  X  /  X  X  X  X  X  X;
```

resulting in the rhythm of another popular (British) football chant. Individuals may arrange a sequence of beats and half-beats for the others to attempt, either travelling, as described above, or clapping.

(9) Court Dances. Step to a piece of music in 4/4 time, altenating left and right feet or sides of the body on the first beats of successive bars, which will result in the rhythms that formed the basis of court and social dances.[49]

(10)Sounds Structured and Free and Silent. The group moves, claps and/or sings a repeated pattern of four beats:[50]

(a) structured — on the beat for the four beats,
(b) free — over a period of four beats, and
(c) silent — for the duration of four beats. Repeat.

The free section will be anarchic; the leader will have to indicate the beginning and end of the silent section. Experiencing the 'electricity' in the silence after the free section reveals an individual's sense of control.[51] Groups of more able individuals have, individually, chosen difficult repeated patterns, e.g. five on the beat, three free and eleven silent, which when performed together resulted in a fascinating chorus-choreography.

(11)Subdivision. A regular pulse is set up in foot-tapping, above which the voice and hands subdivide, exercising duplet, i.e. half-, quarter- or eighth-beats, and triplet, i.e. third- or sixth-beats, as much as possible playing off the main beats: syncopation.[52]

That the presentation of this section might suggest a progression from individual to group rhythms is not to be interpreted as group member superseding individual; the progression could as easily be reversed from structured to free rhythm.

(III)Sound-play: (B) Tune

This section exercises the vertical aspect of music: the pitch of interval. Just as the important rhythmic sensation is time suspended between the pulses, so is the experience of space within the interval, i.e. the change of vibration from one note to the next, intrinsic to music.

(1) Plainsong. The group sustain a drone, above which individuals 'take flight' in sounds, words and hand gestures, contrasting free play of long and short notes with structured regular rhythms and coming to rest on the drone. To assist individuals who have limited sounds, the leader may have to pick up the pitch of the note and gesture and bring them to earth.[53] The principle behind unaccompanied song or plainsong is that the drone is understood.

(2) Chords. The group sustains a note and feels the changes in the body[54] as chords are changed below it, preferably sustained on the organ or accordion, first slowly then quickened. Chord changes may be gradual, e.g.

(a)   I-III or VI, i.e. two notes in common;
(b)   I-IV or V, i.e. one note in common; then
(c)   I-II or VII, i.e. no notes in common.[55]

Songs may be selected with these principles in mind, e.g. (a) Beatles' songs, (b) almost any song, and (c) 'Drunken Sailor'.

(3) Major and Minor. The group sings a song, in major and minor, and the leader inserts suitable verses in the opposite mode.[56]

(4) Blocks of Sound. The leader conducts the group, who sustain notes, changing them as he indicates; or he may play them on the organ or accordion by superimposing as a listening exercise.[57] In previous exercises the pitch of notes might have been aids to memory, e.g.:

(5) Support Music (A5). After standing on a card, accompanied by a chorus, an individual may have the choice of two, three or four cards (of different colours) to step on to, to each of which the group sings a different (generalised) pitch, e.g. high or low, very high or very low, according to his signing.[58]

(6) Football Chant (A8). The original four cards may be 'pitched':

resulting in the final chant rhythm as:[59]

(7) Grunting. Exercise grunting at different pitches. Each group member grunts a note and indicates its pitch in the air, which is repeated by the group. Grunts may be repeated singly at first; then grouped in twos, threes or fours; finally as a whole sequence, phrased in twos, threes or fours.[60]

Articulated Intervals[61]

Certain musical intervals, e.g. 8v, 5th and −3rd, are common in normal communication, and may be effectively exercised in isolation; limiting the pitch may be compensated by inventive use of rhythm and texture.

(8) Octave. Play with the sound of the octave, ascending and descending, by leap and step.[62]

(9) Organum. Sing songs, some verses of which the leader sings or accompanies the 5th below.[63]

(10)Thumb Fifths. Using hand signs, thumb up = 5 and thumb down = 1, the leader improvises rhythmic patterns, e.g.

1 ^{5} ^{5} 1 ^{5} 1 ^{5} 1 1 1 ^{5} 1, etc.

for the group to imitate simultaneously, which creates great fun.[64]

(11)Minor Third. Play calling games utilising the natural calling sound of the falling −3rd.

(12)Within the Interval. The group sings a song, but dwells on each word or note for as long as it takes them to be fully involved in it; then gradually the speed is quickened to normal but still intent upon keeping wholly involved.[65]

Melismatic Intervals

(13)Keening. Improvise a 'lament' by sustaining a note and ornamenting above and below it, sliding from note to note, with hand gestures to help; the interval of the ornament may increase on either side of the held note, e.g.

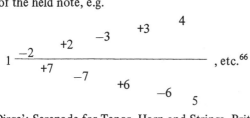

, etc.[66]

cf. 'Dirge': Serenade for Tenor, Horn and Strings, Britten.

(14)Ornamented Folksong. Sing a folksong and ornament it lavishly with melisma, being aware whether the ornaments are melodic, as demonstrated in Keening (13), or harmonic, as below:[67]

(III) Sound-play: (C) Textures

Texture is the 'depth' element of sound[68] against a background of silence.

(1) Tactile Objects. Play with the textures and shapes of visual objects, lingering over a quality as long as is desired,[69] looking at them from different angles and height[70] and trying to translate them into sounds.

(2) Percussive and Sustained Songs. Individuals stand near to slung cymbals to feel the effect of sound on their bodies, and respond to the different effects of banged and rolled sound.[71]

(3) Piano Quintet. A group — of five at the most — sits in front of a piano, which has its front removed and the sustaining pedal depressed or is totally stripped down to the strings, to allow the different qualities of plucked or strummed string sounds to affect their bodies.[72]

(4) Opposites. Explore materials of opposite qualities of texture, e.g. sharp-blunt, hard-soft, cold-warm, heavy-light, oily-gritty, rough-smooth, angular-curved, etc., and try to reproduce these qualities in movement and sounds: sustained-articulated, smooth-percussive, direct-indirect, etc., exercising slow-fast changes between qualities.[73]

The opposite qualities of sound-silence may have been related to the negative-positive cutouts and remnants for a 'lilypond' (extension of B5, Support Music).[74]

(5) The Elements. The floor may be divided into four areas: 'water', 'air', 'earth' and 'sky', which dictate the qualities of sound that individuals may make as they pass through them.

(6) Stereophonic Sound. Groups of different sizes are placed around a room and make sounds producing stereophonic effects, concentrating particularly on feeling the silence between, and choosing between 'nice' and 'nasty' sounds with which to reply, i.e. individual experience of consonance and dissonance.

(7) Calling. Pairs and groups play with sounds of calling from far-near, related to the size of appropriate gestures, big-small. Confusing loud-near, soft-big, etc. causes great fun.[75]

(8) Mirrors. Pairs face each other and move towards and away, attempting to make simultaneous sounds and gestures.[76]

(9) Sound Images. Make up sound images based on textures and qualities (rather than shapes) of, for example, wind, walking, tree, etc., or of characters, for example compounds of heavy, symmetrical, short, indirect, percussive, etc., which are repeated as refrains during the recitation of a story by the leader.[77]

(10)Vowels. Explore rudimentary animal sounds, e.g. 'AH' — contented, 'EE' — screaming, and 'OO' — pouting; then modify them as human sounds, e.g. 'EH' — half-scream, and 'OH' — half-pout: constituting the structure of the five basic or cardinal vowels.[78]

(11) 'Big-bang'. The whole group, each with one sound, possibly played on piano or instrument, together make a loud noise and repeat their notes, individually increasing the length of silence between; this will need to be conducted by the leader from a prepared 'score', possibly on graph paper.[79]

(12)Name Chorus. In a circle, the group sing their names (see I3, Framing), with choices of:
(a) high or low pitch, keeping to a regular pulse;
(b) long or short duration, each individual coming in immediately the one before has finished; and
(c) immediate or delayed entry, as soon as the individual before has opened his mouth to utter, resulting in a chorus of banked sounds and silences.[80]

(IV)Reflection

The climax of the session will have been the creation of a piece of music; each individual and the group will have to some degree presented a bit of themselves and will probably be feeling excited and exposed.[81] They will need to be taken back to normality,[82] taking something of the session, it is to be hoped, to help enrich their lives.[83]

(1) Memory. The leader recalls the events of the session, probably as a link for the following week, as a story[84] in recitative, encouraging moments of group participation, e.g. recalling in sounds the ways they had moved, songs from stories or to cover events, the weather, etc.

(2) Grounding. Sing songs of individual choice, gradually reducing the level of activity and sound to humming and silence.

Acknowledgements

I am extremely indebted to the Carnegie UK Trust who generously funded the project based at Dartington College of Arts, Devon: *The Arts in the Education of Handicapped Children and Young People,* which made it possible for me to: study communication from the other side of normal; to work with Bruce Kent — who was so generous in sharing experiences relating visual art to movement and music, and David Ward — from whose music-making with a very wide range of handicapped children I learnt much about the physicality of music and whose books are compulsory reading for anyone interested in this area of work; and to meet the many teachers, therapists, helpers and artists questioning the boundary between handicapped and non-handicapped people. Special reference must be made to Veronica Sherborne for the illuminating experience of her movement workshops from which many of the body exercises in this writing are adaptations for group and chorus work.

Notes

1. For containment, with the possibility of group member becoming individual, e.g. moving into the circle to perform and possibly be imitated by the group. The area of play, i.e. the space within which to behave beyond the norm, may be defined by instruments, chairs, etc. Low benches proved useful as a 'cat-walk' into a 'circus' from the changing rooms, then angled to define a more manageable space within a large room.

2. 'Individual' may include helper: a physical and vocal extension and interpreter; see (9) Simultaneity, (10) Alternatives, (12) Opposition, (14) Lift, (14) Duplet-triplet, (17) Self and other communication, (21) Reflex and considered action, (29) Breath.

3. Sustained and articulated phrase: IIIA, Rhythm (39).

4. Actions within actions as in a story (84).

5. Occasion to acknowledge sadness; raising status of those present; extending concerns beyond immediate confines; question and answer.

6. Ability to manage silence, vulnerability.

7. Immediate memory exercise; keeping lifted in the silences. *Note*: clapping, i.e. inward arm movement holding on to a feeling reiterated in repeated movements, to be preferred in Shaker form, i.e. hands meeting and opening upwards and outwards.

8. Laughing *at* oneself, *with* the group is socially healthy.

9. Simultaneity, e.g. mirror-image exercise, helps envisaging oneself removed;

imitation from the side when touch or confrontation is impossible.

10.Gesture or signing, paradoxically by taking pressure off the eyes and releasing tension from upper body, allows fuller eye contact.

11.Change of mood at climax; parrot-fashion learning here justified because football chant is social currency; sense of belonging (Chorus: David Ward).

12.Familiarity of communal songs to balance rawer, cruder sounds of creativity. Though still the containing stage of the session, expressive elements introduced through slight modification of regular rhythm, suspended double beat

$$\text{♩ ♩ ♩}$$
$$\text{L R L –,}\qquad\text{R L R – etc.}$$

allows extended reaching: opposition of left and right sides. Reaching arms and extending vowel approximating yawning: maximum longways stretch, anus to soft palate, and sideways, hand to hand, the most lifted sensation in the body, which, sustained, is the basis of singing. With some disturbed groups, repetition of familiar songs might be the extent of the lesson, i.e. confirming manageable space and working within it, but a creative dimension, i.e. listening, play and formalising, is possible in exercising qualities of loud-soft, far-near, e.g. song-dances exploring small-large circles; fast-slow, e.g. song sung at double and triple speeds; major-minor transforming moods.

13.Simple song structure: 'Who has, – Who has, – Who has come into the room': ready-steady-go principle.

14.Means for transforming modes of communication in speech; giving information, generally controlled duplet pulse stresses as opposed to expressing feeling, expansive triplet pulse stresses: a pulse = two or three beats, a stress = two or three syllables; running – duplet: skipping – triplet. Alex, aged 19, who normally walked fast, noticing little, became excited by his self- and environment awareness, being held back by a strong wind; similarly changing duplet into triplet pulse to each step made him more open. Nigel, aged 29, though possessing an extensive repertoire of tunes which he hummed, only grunted isolated sounds. By encouraging the grunt

rebound, 'uh-uh' for a two-syllable work, e.g. 'Daw-lish', then

extending to three, e.g. 'E-xe-ter', I could use the third sound of the triplet as the

first sound of a new stress, e.g. 'O-ver there'. An initial sound, sign or mark may be comparatively easily prompted; the problem is encouraging the individual to react to it to make the second: keeping him alive during the gap.

15.Obsessional rocking, reflex motion, being accepted then extended.

16.Body enclosed in self-communication, humming an extra layer of 'smell'.

17.Erect, retaining self-assurance of curled-up sphere.

18.Sideways movement allowing limitless reaching; long lines of pairs become ships: shipwrecks, underwater movement and sounds.

19.Moment of overbalance in reaching related to suspended beat

$$\text{♩ ♩ → ♩ ♩ ⌣ ♩ ♩ → ♩ ♩ ♩}$$

of duplet becoming triplet (see Note 64):

20.Exercising seesaw for two-way action of communication;

distinguish 'push and be pushed' or 'pull and be pulled' from 'push and pull': reach-recoil reflex action of individuals who compulsively put objects in mouth extended to considered action.

21. Body as self-recognising container and expressor of feelings, self-communication prior to other communication.

22. Exercise sound related to body-movement; music removed fron physicality of dance degenerates into cerebral activity. *Note*: Stravinsky reintegrating music with dance.

23. Singers tuning up; 'M' inward lip-movement; teeth kept apart for free jaw.

24. Important sensation of simple syncopation between pulses on 'big' (or 'little', 'pink', 'brown', etc.), challenging rigidity of pulses; principle applies to time between striking instrument; motivation; compare vowel between consonants. Exercise syncopated clapping:

$$\text{duplet} - \quad \overset{\text{clap}}{\underset{\text{step}}{\times}} \; \overset{}{\times} \; \overset{\text{clap}}{\underset{\text{step}}{\times}} \; \overset{}{\times} \;, \text{ and triplet} - \quad \overset{}{\underset{\text{step}}{\times}} \; \overset{\text{clap clap}}{\times} \; \overset{}{\times} \; \overset{}{\underset{\text{step}}{\times}} \; \overset{\text{clap clap}}{\times} \; \overset{}{\times} \;, \text{ etc.}$$

(See Notes 39 and 64.)

25. Contrast walking on pointed toes, 'lordly', and smooth heels, 'peasant', exercises high and low body-centres producing different qualities of sound, catering for individuals of different dispositions.

26. Sad quality effective at containing, turning-inwards stage of session; song sequence: upwards, heels – knees – back – fingers, and downwards, sides – bottom, makes satisfying arc.

27. Should ideally be experienced in this fast group-regulated version only after individual exploration of cavities' resonances.

28. Drones: warming at body-centre; sense of centre reaffirmed from tension drawn downwards before lifting.

29. (a) Held breath blocking tension in the muscle here exercised in fun normally to be avoided; uncontrolled release of energy in aggressive reflex action may be transformed into considered expression, e.g. expletives – sentences, grunts – songs, kicks – dance steps, hitting – gestures;

(b) Both shallow and deep breathing need exercise; avoid percussive in-out motion, raising tension: instead exercising rolling abdominal movement, i.e. inwards *and* upwards for exhalation and outwards *and* downwards for inhalation;

(c) Extending breath to spread thoughts and feelings out; self – prior to other – recognition.

30. Principle of sentence: a thing (noun) activated (verb); sentence structured based on Who, What happened, When, Where, How and Why; polyrhythm of speech-stresses, i.e. mixture of two and three, essential rhythmic expression in undemonstrative cultures.

31. Full breath release avoids frustration build-up.

32. In social dance, the agreed feet patterns over which real communication is played through eye and upper body contact.

33. The sequence of sound rebound couplet, i.e. 'uh-uh', 'ga-ga', 'da-da', 'ma-ma' and 'ba-ba' trace infant development from amorphous to self-identification.

34. Fascination – commitment; accommodation – assimilation (Piaget).

35. Arts rehabilitating infant sensory deprivation; habit of one-way touch, i.e. handling persists in one-way action of expressing feeling: violence.

36. Noise = inanimate sound. *Note*: 'inanimate' elements becoming effective means of therapy, e.g. swimming, enclosing and fluid sensation; horse-riding, lift of pulse through base of body.

37. Communicating supplements and expressive alternatives; music leaving no

sound record may be compensated by seen elements in action: all media concerned with structuring time and space in forms to compensate touch.

38. A breath = potential step, gesture or sound phrase.

39. A breath phrase may be sustained or broken up, i.e. articulated with a build-up of excitement towards the phrase climax in proportion to the relationship of pulses. However, mechanically regular pulses or beats spell musical death, even within rhythmic patterns of social dance; a triplet should not be based on three even beats, but rather on the principles of the suspended duplet.

40. Transforming antagonism to co-operation, essential exercise.

41. Words, for example, describing direction: 'To George . . . to Val' etc.

42. Two- to three-dimensional exercise in body-image, essential for individuals who feel they are always on display.

43. Opening circle to longways is a crucial learning experience: importance of midway semicircle; compare body opening from self-contained 'sphere' to other-aware erect, by way of 'demi', half-open and enclosed: animal alert, martial artist.

44. Distinction to be made between sounds that: (a) duplicate each step, and (b) (more profitably for extending halting walk) lift the gap between steps, syncopation, motivation; downwards action of step lifts body: consonant conveying vowel.

45. See IIIC, 9, Sound Images: tile patterns convenient for circle – longways.

46. Communication dilemma: to advance or reflect.

47. Related to measuring a room or corridor by using means of mobility.

48. See IIIA, 9, Court Dances.

49. Marching, pounding left foot presumably deadening right brain hemisphere, of Schumann March in 3/4.

50. Experience of rhythms better through sideways movement, i.e. opposition (see Note 12), than clapping (see Note 7).

51. Managing contrast of feelings dependent, ideally, on ability to maintain a sense of centre, or for fast readjustment afterwards.

52. Free section unconscious subdivision; syncopation, sounded or felt.

53. See II6, Rockets.

54. Accommodating response (see Breath, 29).

55. Predominance of I-IV-V chords, progression one note in common, related to minimum of sustaining 'touch'; handicapped people might prefer security of two notes in common.

56. Accommodating change of mood.

57. 'Modern' sound justified by modern composers. Neil, aged 16, having defined his territory on the piano with toys and spit, banged relentlessly at the top on two adjacent white notes, i.e. −2nd nearest to noise on the piano requiring limited response; I tried to join in playing the same notes further down the piano, i.e. less vibration, and grouping in two and three, i.e. opening space, without success. Moving his hands one note, i.e. two white notes with black note between, i.e. +2nd, presumably because of increased interval space, caused him to pause; through gradual play he managed to assimilate this sound; I would have liked to develop this principal working down the intervals of the harmonic scale, i.e. −3rd, +3rd, 4th and 5th, but we lost contact.

58. A group of five people sit at the piano: very low, low, middle, high, very high, and the leader-conductor, facing them, 'conducts' them.

59. Perfect intervals, essential components to vocabulary.

60. Related to building group sentences, one word each, or group stories, one action each (see Note 30).

61. Articulated = jointed, e.g. intervals on piano, guitar; melismatic = clinging (*mele*=honey), e.g. sitar, jazz, folksong ornamentation.

62. Level of formal speaking octave above individual deepest note, i.e. double

vibrations; exercise of which might be the means to inculcate the physical sensation of objectivity.

63. Informal speech range within 5th; I9, Rocking, II3, Toe Song cadence 5-1 may be extended 5-, 5: 5th to 8v.

64. Decrease in waiting for group to catch up, indication of reflex and involvement; hand-signs based on tetrachord: upper of scale 5th above lower half.

65. Normal response simultaneous with changing notes or chords: handicapped people may be too slow or too deep to 'keep up'.

66. Perfect intervals ornamented, e.g. 8 by +7, 5 by −6, 4 by +3 and 1 by −2, produce wild, sensual, 'archaic' mode, opposite to ascetic, 'dorian' mode: 8   −7   +6   5   4   −3   +2   1, favoured in West; range between 'archaic' and 'dorian' has greater subtlety than polarisation of major and minor.

67. 'Grounding' the tune.

68. Terms 'high', 'low', etc. questionable. A blind pianist describing how he learnt part-playing used terms like 'forward', 'back': perspective?

69. Compare with neoclassical practice of Stravinsky and Picasso.

70. Particularly for individuals limited to the height of wheelchairs.

71. Percussive jolt accommodated by gradually increasing tremolo.

72. Relating sustained strumming to percussive plucking.

73. Managing change of moods; centring.

74. Although given limited space here, the experience of listening is in some situations more relevant than activity.

75. Signing, supplementing speech, alleviates tension.

76. Seeing the self removed; moving apart may allow re-enaction of evolution from touch-smell to word images.

77. Recitation allowing words to be sustained in near-singing to hold attention.

78. Include continental 'U' = 'OO' + 'EE', and 'Ø' + 'EH' to exercise facial muscles.

79. Exercise in managing silences, sustaining climax: of aleatory composition.

80. Development of I3, Framing.

81. Post-climax in Greek drama for teaching moral. Just as children may tear up drawings after creating them, so they need time to come to terms after revealing themselves in sound.

82. Timing of programme of sessions (see introduction to the section on music, pp. 108-11), to include time before and after to take group from and return to norm.

83. To help some groups of physically handicapped children be more aware of floor exercise influencing their normal lives I kept them in their chairs, extending their activities until they felt they needed to move to the floor; being returned, they could recapture what they had done, particularly if there was the visual record of a 'map' of their wanderings (marked in individual colours) translated into songs and stories. With other groups, exercises were repeated in different positions, e.g. on the floor, half-erect and fully erect, or sitting, standing and moving, to reinforce their value.

84. Exercising sense of structure; story taking listeners out of themselves following a narrative and reflecting on the events.

9 DRAMA: USING THE IMAGINATION AS A STEPPING-STONE FOR PERSONAL GROWTH

Bernie Warren

For many people drama is something that happens on a stage, a stage that separates the performers from the audience, and establishes the people presenting events to the people watching them as skilled 'craftsmen'. Yet this presentation of 'imagined acts'[1] on a stage is simply one facet of dramatic activity and although it is perhaps the most generally accepted view of what 'drama' is, it is not necessarily the most important. It is this misconception in many people's minds, that drama is only a presentation on a stage and thus the sole property of skilled and talented individuals, that has created blocks in allowing individuals to achieve their full creative potential, and in some cases even prevents their imaginations from coming into play at all. It is against this often self-imposed wall that professionals in the fields of developmental drama, personal creativity and drama therapy have been chipping away for more than two decades.

Drama, in common with other art forms, almost certainly had its origins in ritual.[2] In most cases, spontaneous actions precede ritual. In the creation of ritual these spontaneous actions, which are seen to have meaning for the well-being of the group, become transformed into a symbolic act. It now becomes essential for the original spontaneous actions to be carried out in a set order and with a particular style. This specific pattern is believed to be essential to the ritual 'working' and, as a result, spontaneity is lost.[3] This is a similar process to the one most people have, consciously or unconsciously, pursued with their own creativity. They have lost contact with their source of spontaneity and have fallen back on external frameworks which impose boundaries on the imagination and, more disastrously, often totally remove any emotional reaction and substitute it with conscious control.

Drama rarely, if ever, occurs in isolation. Individuals may occasionally indulge in isolated dramatic actions[4] but, for drama to occur, more than one person has to be present. Drama is an example of human interaction. It is concerned with human beings communicating with one another; verbally, physically and emotionally. Most importantly, this dramatic interaction is part of our everyday lives. Many role-theorists[5] have pointed out that we are constantly shifting roles. Earlier in this book, Rob Watling elaborates on the way in which context and function affect traditional material. In a similar way the roles we take are influenced by their context – e.g. where we are, who we are talking to, etc. – and their function. Thus the roles we take are often dictated by circumstances beyond our control.

Perhaps the most important external influences on our often unconscious role-playing are the people with whom we interact. In everyday interactions it is not just what we say, but how we say it that conveys not only our meaning but also our feelings, and preceding every action there is thought, sometimes subconscious, which in turn is inextricably linked to the imagination. Our every action, nuance of inflection and gesture are recorded, sometimes subliminally, by the people with whom we communicate. They then calibrate[6] their actions and the roles they take accordingly. I believe that in this process is encapsulated the essence of drama. For me, drama is about the process whereby 'imaginative thought becomes action'[7] – in word or deed – and is particularly concerned with the way that this 'dramatic action' affects others. In essence, drama can be thought of as the communication of our imagination, through our action in a way which affects our interactions with others, whether this be on stage or in our daily lives.

One of our biggest problems on our daily stage is in communicating what we mean. Every one of us spends a large part of our day talking at but not necessarily communicating with others. I often draw the analogy of human beings being transceivers (transmitter/receivers). I feel that we all transmit on a 'wavelength' specific to us. We have our own 'radio station', which is created by, among other things, our past experience, our vocabulary and our world map.[8] Although we can transmit only on this one station,[9] we have the capacity to receive an incoming 'signal' on almost any wavelength. The problem is that all too often, in our struggles to communicate, we are not tuned in properly – we are not quite 'on station' – so we pick up only some of the incoming signal. Frequently we are not listening because we are too busy working on our next 'broadcast', on what we are going to say. As a result, we miss the point or lose the feeling of what the person talking to us is saying.

This process relates to all human communications. As I sit writing these words, displaced both in time and space from you reading them, I am struggling to find those words which will best convey my meaning to you. I am well aware that what I write, on the basis of my language system and world map, will have to be interpreted by you and that every reader will have a widely differing, unique background. So, as I write, I am calling on my imagination, trying to be aware of who will be reading these words, what their backgrounds are and what, if any, common ground they share. I am at the beginnings of the dramatic process. I am struggling to communicate and my imagination is *affecting* my actions. I am searching for the mode by which I can be heard by as many readers as possible, and in the process I am having to review the roles I have taken to transmit my meaning in my past.

Drama is concerned with communication between people. Many of the people we work with have difficulty communicating. Much of this results from an inability to change roles or response to an alteration in external circumstances. This lack of role-flexibility[10] may be a result of a number of interrelated factors, e.g. poor language use, inadequate body control, emotional blocks, poor social skills, etc. These factors often conspire to maintain an individual's inability to respond to external changes.

Through drama, individuals can not only be allowed to use their imaginations, but can also be encouraged to enjoy using them. Through games, improvisations and theatre scripts, different roles[11] can be taken. It is through this role-play and character-work that individuals can start to imagine what it is like to *be* someone else. These imaginative leaps can, through enactment and discussion of well-known job roles, e.g. teacher, farmer, lawyer, policeman, etc., engender a greater understanding of social roles, or through similar enactment and discussion of more personal material, as in psychodrama,[12] lead to a greater awareness of one's self and one's relationship to family, friends and past life.

It is through dramatic process, by playing[13] other roles and through engaging imaginations and emotions, that we can increase our role-flexibility, develop our powers of communication and learn to interact acceptably in the society in which we live.

Practical Activities

Like all the arts, drama is a personal activity. Developing your own personal style and making the material used your 'own' — so it fits your way of working — is often as important as the material itself. My own style is generally light, particularly in the early stages of a group's life, and my role is that of actor/facilitator.[14] Anyone who has worked with me will tell you of the strong emphasis I place on humour as a vehicle for engaging other emotions. I place great store on gaining my group's trust and confidence through humour, laughter and enjoyment. My work as a clown and a comic actor obviously stands me in good stead for this. My reasons for sharing this with the reader are two-fold. First, readers can look at my style of presentation and try to relate it to their own, but, more importantly, I share this information because I feel that without an element of fun, enjoyment and spontaneity many of the other benefits will not be reached. Engaging the interest of individuals in the group precedes gaining their confidence, and without their confidence and trust, no matter how much training and experience you have had, they will be extremely reticent to share their world — with all its hopes, fears and emotions — with you. So no matter what your style, a primary concern is engaging and keeping the group's interest. It was with this in mind that I chose the following material. All of the material is 'track tested' and requires little or no equipment. I have divided the material into three sections: Name Games, Awakening the Imagination, and finally Story-telling/Character Creation.

Name Games

In the beginning an individual's name is perhaps the most important thing he* brings with him into the dramatic arena. For some of the people I work with their name is the only thing they can share with the group and some find even this too much for them. Our name is our identity, it tells others who we are and reaffirms our own existence. Name games allow the group to get to know one another and establish a sense of group spirit. I generally play a name game at the beginning of each session, just to re-establish the group. This is particularly important if the group meets once a week or less. Name games also allow each individual to be spotlighted,[15] i.e. for a short period of time individual participants are the centre of attention. A name game sets the tone of 'we as a group are here and we all have names, personalities, feelings — we are all individuals'.

Simple Name Game(s). Initially this game and its many variations are best played sitting in a circle. The leader starts by saying his name and then asks each person to say his own name in turn around the circle. This saying of names can go first to the right and then to the left of the leader, all the way round the circle.

A variation is for the leader to point at the person who has to speak

*Please note that I use the pronoun 'he' throughout this chapter to denote men or women. I have done this for reasons of simplifying linguistic style.

— this can sometimes be threatening, particularly with a new group. Another variation is for the leader to walk around the inside of the circle, stopping in front of each group member and saying 'My name's Bernie, and what's your name?' On the reply, e.g. 'My name's Susan', the leader and Susan would shake hands. This continues until the leader has introduced himself to all of the group.

Mr Engine. Mr Engine is a variation on shaking hands. It is a children's game I learnt from Bert Amies that is full of sound, ritual and enjoyment. The group sits in a circle with the leader standing in the centre. The leader is the engine of the train — known as 'Mr Engine'. As the engine moves he makes steam train noises, e.g. 'Choo choo choo choo, Choo choo choo choo' and when he comes to a halt in front of one of the group members, he goes 'Woo woo', making an action as if pulling on a lever. There then follows a ritual exchange. The engine starts 'Hello, little girl'; hopefully the girl replies 'Hello, Mr Engine'; leader 'What's your name?', reply 'My name is Sue'; leader to rest of group 'Her name is Sue', to Sue 'Would you like to join my train, Sue?'; reply (hopefully) 'Yes, please.' At this point Sue 'joins the train' by standing behind the engine and putting her arms around Mr Engine's waist. Slowly, the number of 'cars' behind Mr Engine increases, each linking around the waist of the car in front. When the engine has cars added, the name of the new person is said by each member of the train with the last car saying that name to the rest of the group. So if the train with two cars stops in front of Brian, the ritual goes like this: engine to first car 'His name is Brian'; first car to second car 'His name is Brian. (pause) Would you like to join our train, Brian?' In this way the person's name is passed down the train and the greater the number of cars the train has, the more times the name is said. This repetition of the person's name acts as a form of spotlighting and the extended repetition in some ways compensates for being one of the last cars to join the train. However, it is very important that the last people to join are made to feel part of the group.

The structure of the game allows for full group involvement at all stages of its development. There are the ritual chants with all the group accompanying the leader on the 'Choo choo choo choo, Choo choo choo choo' and on the 'Woo Woo, Woo Woo'. The group members can physically become the moving train and when the whole group is part of the train, a song can be sung as the train moves around the room, in and out of the furniture. One of my favoured songs is 'Chatanooga Choo Choo'.

This is a great game to get people involved, out of their chairs and moving. If you have the luxury of volunteers,[16] try to intersperse them between the people who might need assistance. Occasionally people will refuse to join the train but a little gentle persuasion is often all that is needed. In the case of someone obstinately refusing to join the train, try *not* to spend undue time attempting to coax them because you risk losing the attention of other members of the group. After moving as a unit, the train can uncouple one car at a time; again this can be accompanied by a song or a group chant. This game is a good way of separating and mixing group members.

Dracula. This is one of my favourite games. It is also one that is asked for over and over again by groups of all ages and abilities. Over the years this game has changed quite considerably, mainly as a result of the groups who have played it.

At the start of the game the group sits in a circle and I stand in the middle. I ask the group about vampires and Dracula. After a very brief discussion, I tell them that I am going to be Dracula, one of the 'undead', and that they are all in the land of the living. I tell them that Dracula can return to the land of the living only if he can find a victim to take his place. Dracula does this by means of an 'instant blood exchange' through placing his fangs (Dracula's index fingers) at the back of his victim's neck. The victim then becomes the new Dracula. Sometimes I tell them that Dracula's spirit is always in need of a new host body to avoid the ravages of time – this adds to the blood exchange idea.

However, Dracula doesn't have it easy! As Dracula walks towards his victims, finger fangs outstretched, the intended victim makes the sign of the cross (by crossing index fingers). As soon as the sign of the cross is made, the rest of the group shouts the victim's name. If they are successful and call the victim's name prior to Dracula touching his neck, then Dracula must go in search of another victim. If Dracula gets there first, then the victim and Dracula change places and the group has a new Dracula.

Once the group has the general idea of how to play the game, extra rules can be added. Here are *some* examples:

(a) Dracula can be given a 'handicap', e.g. he has to walk with a limp, take baby steps, close one eye, count to three in front of the victim, etc.
(b) The victim has to direct his 'cross' at *one* member of the group

who then has to call the victim's name.

(c) Adding on to (b), if that one member of the group is too slow, it is he, not Dracula's victim, who becomes the new Dracula.

This is a great game for generating eye contact, group feeling and emotional response. Some important points to watch: young children can occasionally be scared by Dracula; always play a simple name game before Dracula; beware of violent Draculas (poking in the back of the neck can hurt!); be prepared to allow Dracula to 'suck blood' from the victim's knees, particularly important for Draculas in wheelchairs.

My final point about Dracula concerns equipment. I now play this game with the added extra of a cape — Dracula's cape — a black one with a scarlet red inner lining. This has really added to the game. It allows Dracula to gain added movement by using the cape's material, it seems to enable the more reticent individuals to 'become' Dracula and it allows for a social exchange between Dracula and victim. At the point of transformation when Dracula has caught a victim, the old Dracula helps the new Dracula on with the cape prior to sitting down as a member of the land of the living. This Transylvanian valet service is often one of the comic highlights of the game.

Tarzan. This is another one of my favourite and most asked-for games. It is often the first name game I play with a new group. I always tell a story before the game, about Tarzan swinging through the jungle and filling it with the sound of his own name. The story can take a number of turns and has a number of explanations for the famous Tarzan call with the explanation changing to meet the needs of the group I am working with.

The basic game is to go round the circle and ask each person's name. This is generally done in both directions. Then I tell the Tarzan story and say that we are going to fill the room with the sound of our names. We then go round the circle, stopping at each group member, who says his name. This is then echoed by the rest of the group shouting that name while beating their chests. This goes all the way round the circle until everyone's name has filled the room, and finally we all beat our chests and shout the Tarzan call.

This is a great game for spotlighting individuals. Even the shyest person's face lights up when they hear all the group shouting his name and that sound filling the room.

These have been but a few examples from the huge array of simple and dramatic name games available in the literature. Often a group will have special, favourite name games. These may be ones you have introduced or, more likely, ones they have adapted or created.

Awakening the Imagination

Many of the people we work with have been actively discouraged from using their imaginations. Programmes that emphasise socially acceptable behaviours and the facing of reality — in the programmer's terms — cause the often fertile imaginations of individuals in our groups to atrophy! I am not suggesting that individuals should not be helped to face the realities of our often inhumane and alienating industrialised society; what I am suggesting is that there are many ways in which this can be achieved. One of these is through the individual's imagination. I feel that to help them grasp a sense of the socially accepted norms of reality, we must first gain a sense of how they imagine the world, and attempt to see the world through their eyes so that we do not always transfer or project our world view on to them. Our understanding of their perceptions of the world, gained through imaginative exercises, can provide a framework in which to initiate a change to more socially acceptable behaviour. The first three games deal with awakening and engaging the senses, and the others in this section focus on the act of creating *something* from *nothing*, and on the imagination taking a concrete object and transforming it into something else.

Keeper of the Keys. A variation on a traditional children's game. I tell the group a story about a pirate who amasses great wealth and keeps this in his house. However, the pirate is often away from his home and needs someone to guard his house and treasure. He is told of a blind man whose hearing is so acute he can hear a pin drop in a crowded room. After an embellished preamble, one of the group sits on a chair in the centre of the circle, closes his eyes and becomes the blind man. The rest of the group is seated in a circle around him. In front of the blind man are the keys to the treasure; for children this is often described as a huge store of candy or chocolate. The rest of the group try, one at a time, to take the keys without being heard. When the blind man hears a noise he points in the direction of the noise, saying 'Get out of this house.' If the would-be-thief is pointed at, he has to go back to his seat. If he captures the keys without being 'spotted', he becomes the new blind man.

Added complications can be to give the blind man a gun (extended index finger) and for him then to say 'Get out of this house — bang!'

This adds the dramatic element of a theatrical death. The thief can be required to get the keys from under the blind man's nose and back to his seat, or a group of two or three thieves can work as a team to get the keys from the blind man (this can be *very* unsettling for the blind man and should not be tried early on).

This game is extremely good for accentuating auditory skills. It is also an exercise in control for the thief, trying not to be heard, and also for the rest of the group who must remain quiet and still.

There is a tendency for the blind man not to keep his eyes totally closed; however, I am reluctant to use a blindfold. My own experience is that many individuals are scared by wearing a blindfold. The return to trust − trusting the individual to keep his eyes closed − requires patience and a liberal dose of turning a blind eye in the initial stages. Slowly, individuals will be less scared of closing their eyes and will become totally engaged in the game. Pushing and cajoling them to close their eyes will probably only aggravate the problem.

Male or Female. This game is a regular favourite. I have found it particularly good when working with groups of long-stay institutionalised people and with psycho-geriatric individuals, as it seems to provide that essential element of acceptable human contact so often lacking from these people's lives.

The group sits in a circle with one member of the group sitting in the middle. The person in the middle has his eyes closed. One at a time other members of the group go and gently touch the person in the centre, who then has to guess whether he was touched by a man or a woman. I never force anyone either to sit in the centre or to get up and touch the person sitting there. I let the game continue until everyone who wants to has had a go.

This game provides a fascinating experience. When you are in the middle it is extremely difficult to discern if the touch is that of a man or a woman; *however*, it does force you to be aware of other factors, e.g. pressure, warmth, sound − particularly breathing. After a while, when working with a group over a long period of time, I can generally pick out exactly who is touching me by the sounds they make coming towards me, their breathing pattern, the way they touch me and so on. As an observer, the ways that people approach the person in the middle and then make physical contact can be particularly informative concerning the dynamics of the group. Often, individuals hide their feelings behind the words they use to communicate; in this exercise these feelings are made concrete, often in very subtle ways.

This activity can also be used as part of work on sex roles and stereo-types. Often, when working with teenagers, a discussion is an essential close to this activity. Other groups, particularly those involving mentally handicapped people, often turn this game into a competition and some individuals get bitterly disappointed if they guess incorrectly. This disappointment needs to be dissipated either through group support or a 'success' in another activity, or whatever means is appropriate to that individual in your group.

This is generally one of the first physical contact activities I use with a group as it gives me a rough gauge of how individuals in the group respond to being touched. It also gives a pointer as to who will/ will not work well together. This activity can lead into more directed activities dealing with emotion and physical contact.

Parachute. In my work I use very little in the way of equipment. However, I always carry a parachute around with me. The quality of the material, the feeling of group contact and the sensation of movement to be gained from working with a parachute are unequalled by anything I have yet experienced.

There are many different parachute games and I use a number of parachute exercises, all for different purposes. This exercise is one linked to sensation. The group stands in a circle. If there are a number of individuals in wheelchairs, I start by sitting in a circle. Everybody holds on to the parachute with both hands, if this is possible. We then try to work as a group, raising the parachute as high as it will go and then letting it return to the floor. I try to get the group to work together, working towards the rise and fall of the parachute becoming smooth and rhythmic.

When the group has achieved this rhythmic flow, I ask each person to say a word or sentence to describe what the parachute makes them feel. I ask them to say this when the parachute is at the top of its travel. This allows that individual to make eye contact with other members of the group. I then ask the group to repeat the word or sentence as the parachute returns to the floor. Sometimes the feeling described is a simple emotion, e.g. happy; sometimes the feeling described is a sensation evoked by the movement of the parachute, e.g. light and airy. In this way not only do participants express the sensations they feel, but they are also exposed to new vocabulary. In addition to working on linking sensation to expression, the parachute is an excellent tool for extending physical limits.[17]

The Magic Box. Anyone who has ever worked with me knows I always carry with me a large magic box. On the outside, painted in large letters, are the words 'Bernie's Magic Box'. This box has a practical purpose, as it enables me to carry with me all the equipment I ever use — tape recorder, tapes, parachute, etc. However, it has another far more important function and that is to serve as a focus for group members' imaginations.

The magic box is an extremely simple tool. It is one of those timeless dramatic activities. Stanislavski used a version of the magic box for training actors, and many noted individuals working in drama have some form of magic box exercise. In essence the magic box is a projective exercise. All I ask as leader is 'What do you think is in the box?' The group then responds by projecting from their imaginations what they think is in the box. The responses of the group can then be directed or shaped by the leader in a number of ways.

In the first instance I generally employ a *free association* approach — where I simply allow the group to come up with as many ideas as possible. When using this approach I try not to make judgements, although I do make mental notes of who said what. Also, I attempt to provide an environment that allows the group to imagine as many things to be inside the box as they want to tell me about.

Sometimes I am slightly more directive, taking a *theme-based* approach. Here I tell the group there is food or treasure or unusual objects inside the box. This is an approach I take with mentally handicapped youngsters. I still allow the group to free-wheel, but within a given framework. This can provide the necessary grounding for individuals who are 'paralysed' by a completely open-ended task.

Sometimes I break with a free-wheeling or free-association approach and take a *question-based* approach. Here, as soon as an individual has a particular idea about what is in the box, I ask questions related to the object they have described. For example, if they have suggested there is a purse in the box, I might ask, 'What colour is it?' 'How large is it?' 'Is it soft?' 'Does it have writing on the outside?' and so on. As a result of these questions, often a clear picture of this object can be created in a very short space of time.

Once the group has created objects, there are a number of ways of working with the ideas. Here are two basic approaches. Having created a variety of objects to be found in the box, take the 'imagined' objects from the box one at a time and pass them round the group. Get the group to take the time to feel each object's texture, weight, etc. At some point I might ask one of the group to describe the object to the rest of the group.

Another technique is to use two or three objects which the group created that might link together. For example, one group told me that in the box, among other things, were a bloody hand, a sword and a dragon's tooth. I then asked the group to tell me how the objects got there. In this way, from the objects a group creates, a story can evolve, which can then be 'acted out'. The magic box then, in common with other activities described in this section, allows the group to use its collective experience as the basis for the dramatic activity. I will pursue these ideas through description of other activities in this chapter. The magic box can also be used to reinforce the magical qualities of objects that are taken out of it, such as the Magic Newspaper.

Magic Newspaper. This is one of my 'old faithfuls', which I use at some point in my work with every group. This game is both a starting point for mime and also a diagnostic tool.

I produce from my magic box the magic newspaper. I tell the group that this may look like an ordinary newspaper, but it is in fact magic. At this point most of the group is, to say the least, sceptical. I say that the magic of the newspaper is that, by working with it, the paper can become anything you want and that, without telling anyone, the group will immediately know what it is. I then create a telescope, someone in the group says 'telescope', I reply 'See, magic works every time', and we're off. I then might show a few more examples of the newspaper's power and then the paper is passed around the circle. Each person has a chance to work with the 'magic'. The only rule is that you cannot pass twice. So if you cannot think/make something first time round, you must do something the next time.

The way that individuals respond to the magic newspaper is fascinating and it is for me, as already mentioned, a very valuable diagnostic tool. From the way individuals use the paper I can gain information which enables me to make assumptions about the way their imaginations function. In general terms, given the magic news-paper, there are three basic ways of working with it — moving from the concrete to the abstract use of imagination. In the first instance, people work at a concrete level. The focus is on *making* the newspaper into something. Here the paper has to be an actual representation, e.g. a hat, an aeroplane or a newspaper. What work the individual does with the paper is related to origami. Further along, people reach a stage where they are less concerned about what the object looks like and more concerned about how to use it. The focus is on *using* the newspaper as something, e.g. a paint brush, a baseball bat or a fishing rod. This marks a mid-point between the concrete and the abstract uses of the news-paper. At the most abstract level, the focus is on the newspaper *being part of* a larger imaginative picture, e.g. the newspaper is the lead for a dog being taken for a walk. The focus is now on the dog *not* on the lead. The shift of focus on the newspaper is from making into, to using as, to being part of something − it is a shift from the concrete to the abstract use of imagination. The way the individuals use the paper can serve as a guide to the level at which other imaginative exercises might best be started.

Although the ways in which people use the newspaper is a clue to the way in which they use their imaginations, it is by no means a direct cause-and-effect relationship. People who are able to function at the highest abstract level are often intimidated during the first sessions of the magic newspaper and appear to function only at a concrete level. Also, some people appear to be functioning at a higher, more abstract level than would at first be expected. There may also be some who can only copy others. All of these pieces of information should be made note of and used to help fill out the three-dimensional jigsaws that are the individuals within your group. No single piece alone can complete the picture but every little piece of information helps.

Magic Clay. This is an extension of the magic newspaper. Once again it can be a starting point for mime work and in fact I was first intro-duced to this exercise early on in my training as part of a mime work-shop. The workshop leaders showed this as a Pantomime Blanche exercise, which allowed the Mime to 'produce' objects on stage with a minimum of fuss and effort. Magic Clay is my reworking of that simple exercise.

I tell the group that I have a ball of magic clay and that when I work with it I can create objects. I then stretch the clay, drawing it out and shaping it, perhaps into a bouquet of flowers which I then present to someone in the group. When we have completed our transac-tion, I mould the clay back into a ball and pass it to the person next to me. The clay is passed around the circle with each person *consciously* creating something, using/demonstrating it so that the group under-stands, and returning it to the shape of a ball. In this stage of the exercise the ball is being consciously shaped and manipulated by the group member holding it.

Another way of using the magic clay is to ask the person holding it to close his eyes and let the clay move him. The sceptics among my readers will argue that something that does not exist cannot move the individual not holding it. In a sense they are right, yet what is being asked is for the person holding the clay to try to suspend the cerebral override that we all employ in almost any task and let the subconscious take over. The need is to *do*, without thinking about what to do. The results can be fascinating. I ask individuals to describe their experiences as they are happening – telling the rest of the group the colours, shapes, weight, textures, etc. of their experience with the clay. I always emphasise there is not a need to describe or label what has been created, as the end of the process does not have to be something known or tangible.

When the individual lets go of conscious control of the clay, the emotions and the feelings take over. There must be no criticism or judgement of the creation – this is not a work of art, this is a work of emotion, colour and form. The effect of the experience on the individual varies immensely, depending on their emotional state and the degree to which they allow themselves to go with the clay. In most cases people describe it as a relaxing, refreshing and pleasant experience. For others it can act as a stimulus to open the floodgates for troublesome or unresolved past experiences. It is essential that you are aware of this possibility and timetable Magic Clay so that there is always time to explore anything that comes up as a result of the exercise and you do not simply close the session with the activity. This activity integrates well with various visual arts techniques, e.g. 'painting' the experience *with* the clay.

Story-telling/Character Creation

Story-telling has always had an important role to play in the preservation and development of a culture. As has already been pointed out earlier in this book, traditionally story-tellers were held in great esteem and could hold an audience captive for long periods with the tales they spun. Today, with the development of instant and often instantly forgettable culture, there is still a great need for story-tellers. This need is particularly great in the education and development of children. As more and more children are educated primarily through organised schooling and through television, there becomes an even stronger need to re-establish communication with older relatives, e.g. grandparents, aunts, uncles, etc. These older generations can make an invaluable contribution to a child's development, simply by taking the time to tell it stories, putting it back in contact with its heritage, its family's history, in a way that no television programme or film ever can. Flesh and blood relatives retelling tales of their youth can allow the child to be engaged in the experience, and the story-teller can relive those sensations and emotions in such a way that he can actually rebuild the story.

Story-telling and the creating of characters, the act of becoming someone else, are the natural extensions of awakening the imagination. It is this dramatic awakening, the linking of words to emotion, that also forms the backbone for many of the verbal forms of individualised counselling and therapy. In the act of suspending conscious control, in the removing of those blocks that prevent us from being truly creative, we regain contact with the raw emotions, past experiences and inspiration that are the source of the personal creative statement – the unique creative thumbprint that only we as individuals can make. These blocks are the death of personal creativity. We all have them and we all employ them. They allow us to hide behind a wall. They also act as barriers to the human actor acting on the stage of everyday life, fully creating the role that allows him truly to communicate. In my work I have identified what I believe to be three major blocks to being spontaneous and creative. I feel they are present in all of us and are in many ways a necessary defence in certain social situations. However, they are often more apparent in people who have limited role-flexibility and communication skills. I call the three major blocks:

(a) *The wall.* Here, conscious control is so great and people are so desperately trying to be creative that they cannot do anything. A common response is 'I had lots of ideas but when it was my turn to do something, my mind went blank.'

(b) *The censor.* Here, people are able to do something but it is feeble, half-hearted. If questioned, common responses are 'I thought that was what you wanted' or, more importantly, 'I didn't know what others would think.'

(c) *Playing the crowd.* Here, the exhibited behaviour is of someone frantically creating. It is, however, surface behaviour – attention seeking. The individual will use any means of being the centre of the group's attention. At the extreme, there is *no* censoring behaviour, often 'taboo' subjects are played up, with emphasis on cheap laughs and crowd reinforcement.

In exercises/games where the awakened imagination develops a story and later creates characters, these three blocks are particularly prevalent.

The skilled leader can make use of the blocks, first, by making note of them and later, often in the same session, providing material that allows a chance for the individual to overcome them.

Story-telling is not only about linking events, but also often provides a three-dimensional map of where an individual has come from, where he is going to and, sometimes, where he stopped along the way. The construction of the sentences, the inflexion, and the body posture are every bit as important as the content. The leader must be all eyes and ears, sensing the sub-text of what is said. In carefully listening to, observing and developing the events during the session, the leader is able not only to establish a creative environment, but also to help individuals regain contact with themselves and thus start to increase role-flexibility and communication skills.

Tennis-Elbow-Foot Game. In England there is a radio show called 'I'm Sorry, I Haven't a Clue'. It is billed as an anti-panel game and it has some excellent non-quiz games. The tennis-elbow-foot game is one of them. This is my own adaptation of what is basically a cross between Freudian free association and every foolish panel game ever broadcast on radio in England.

The group sits in a circle. The idea is to throw a nerf ball from one person to another. As the ball is thrown, the thrower says a word, for example 'tennis'. The catcher must then respond with the first word that comes into his head, for example 'elbow', simultaneously throwing the ball to another person as they do so. The game is based on an instant response to the word that went before. There should be no time to pre-plan because you never know what word you will have to respond to. If there is a break in continuity or if someone pauses before responding, blocking has almost certainly occurred.

This is an extremely interesting and often entertaining game. It is an excellent exercise to work against blocking and as such to promote spontaneity and creativity. It forms a good springboard for story-telling exercises. It can give valuable clues about individuals within the group in much the same way as the magic box. With mentally handicapped people or young children it is often best to start with a theme, such as colours. So the task would then be to 'say the first colour that you think of'. Once again, it is important to cross-reference information. For example, if a child is stuck with the response 'yellow', certain questions need to be answered. Does he also repeatedly choose yellow in art work? Does he describe their house as yellow? If he does, why? Is it the only colour he knows? Some more deep-seated reason? It is important to gain as much first-hand information as possible, but it is also important to cross-refer experiences with the other professionals who work with that individual.

Earlier in the book I have made reference to the importance of the contract between the leader and the group. If the contract is a 'therapeutic' one, then the leader will want to make note of the *pattern, repetition* and *blocking* of responses for, on the basis of this and information from other activities and sources, an 'intervention' or 'strategy for change' can be planned. In the context above the *pattern* is the sequence of words exchanged between group members, e.g. ON TOP → UNDERNEATH → BLANKET → BED; *repetition* is where an individual is stuck with a particular word or limited response, e.g. purple or only words related to touch; and *blocking* is what occurs when an individual is not able to respond to a particular word or topic, such as love.

The reasons for the patterns, repetition or blocking can be many. One aberration that should be taken into consideration when looking at the pattern is whether individuals were responding to the penultimate word. This happens when the game is being played fast and the group members are new to each other.

Repetition is usually an individual problem and may simply be a language deficiency; this is particularly likely with mentally handicapped people. However, with a more 'verbal' group the repetition *may* be psychological in origin.

Blocking is far more complicated and highlights the problems posed by evaluating the group's responses. Certain words or topics, for example sexuality, may be blocked for a number of individual or collective reasons. One of the most obvious is that individuals feel a lack of trust and confidence in other members of the group. The reasons for this lack of trust may be a key to the direction a strategy for change should take.

In general terms, it is unusual for a group of post-pubescent people not to mention sex − covertly or overtly − at some point in the game. In fact with adolescents, given a supportive and creative environment, the pattern may be predominantly concerned with sex. This can lead to very interesting discussions after the game.

Guided Fantasy.[18] The term 'guided fantasy' is one that is used loosely to describe a leader relating to an individual or group a pertinent tale, anecdote or similar stimulus. At its simplest, the guided fantasy has been the stock in trade of all good story-tellers since humankind first started telling stories. At its central core is the need to engage individuals in the events of the story. Therefore there is a need to choose material that is specific not only to the group's needs but also to their way of viewing the world.

As already mentioned by Rob Watling earlier in this book, traditional material with its store of wisdom and knowledge may often be a suitable starting point for a guided fantasy. The way a story or stimulus is used by a leader can take a number of directions, with the direction often being dictated by the nature of the intended outcome of the exercise.

In a guided fantasy I see the leader's role as being directive or non-directive, and the participants may be actively or passively involved. In a *non-directive* approach the leader simply provides a loose framework — suggestions to stimulate the imagination. In a *directive* approach the leader makes statements that give step-by-step instructions — literally guiding the imagination. These styles are often mixed, so that statements, such as 'You walk down the road and come to a big house. You walk up to the front door', may be interspersed with questions. 'What colour is the door?' 'Is the door open?' The leader may even leave the end totally open for individuals to supply the conclusion that meets their needs.

The participants in a guided fantasy may be *passive*, i.e. relaxed, lying on the floor, eyes closed. The leader may use terms such as 'imagine you are looking at a large cinema screen' — suggesting that the story is happening there and then on the screen, or reference may be made to an environment: 'You are in a garden full of flowers — brightly coloured, beautiful, sweet-smelling — take time to smell the flowers, feel their texture, look at the colours.' The emphasis may then be placed on action or sensation or both.

In a guided fantasy where the participants are *active*, they *do* what the story suggests. Thus, if the story calls for the heroine to ride into town, the participants act as if they were riding into town. If it calls for the heroine to pick a magical flower, the participants act as if they are picking that flower. When participants are active, they are like actors responding to the instructions in the script — they are wide awake and respond in their own creative way within the restrictions imposed by the script.

Sometimes a guided fantasy may be both active and non-directive. When used with a group this is often referred to as a community exercise. Guided fantasy, as with so many other creative activities, is often a stepping-stone to the discussion it creates as a result of participants being engaged in the activity. This discussion is often as important as the activity that preceded it.

To Be Continued (Group Story-telling). This is an excellent way to create a script or story that has significance for the group. The story created can be recorded by means of a tape recorder. It can then be written down and used as a stimulus for other activities, and can be used as a guided fantasy, a theatre script or a starting point for developing reading and writing skills.[19]

The group sits in a circle. The leader starts a story going, e.g. 'Once upon a time in a large city lived a small cat called Boots.' This first sentence is then built on, a section at a time, by each member of the circle, one at a time, contributing to the story − a word, a phrase, a sentence or whatever seems appropriate. Slowly the group introduces new characters and situations, which develop the action. The focus may shift dramatically as a result of characters and situations introduced by the group. What is important is that each group member is actively involved in creating the story − it is an expression of their shared, collective experiences and imaginations.

To spice the activity up, with a group who have had experience in creating their own stories, I take a nerf ball and ask individuals, when they have added their section to the story, to throw the ball to someone else. This makes contributions more spontaneous because you never know when it will be your turn.

Another variation is to have someone in the centre acting out the story as it is being created. I have a rule that they can sit back in the circle at any time and choose who will replace them. Again, you never know when it will be your turn to be in the centre of the circle. The 'actor' often decides to swap with a 'story-teller' when the addition to the story is difficult for them to perform. This leaves the 'story-teller' forced to take his own medicine, normally to the great amusement of the rest of the group.

It is important that less verbal people are allowed to contribute at their own level. For some mentally handicapped people this may require the leader asking questions, some of which a court of law might view as leading the witness. In order that each individual can participate, other individuals may require the leader to intervene to prevent one person controlling the story for an extended length of time. This person is an obvious candidate to be 'the actor' when the time comes to act out the story.

I'm Sorry I Must Be Leaving. This is a standard acting improvisation, which is often a riot to watch. I start a scene with one person in a given situation, such as watching TV, a second person enters and chooses his character, and a scene starts to develop through improvisation. At some point in the scene a third person joins the action. At this point the first person must find a legitimate excuse to leave the scene.

Each time a new 'actor' joins the scene the first person in the scene must leave. Thus, when number four joins the scene, number two must leave and when number five joins, then number three must leave, and so on. The effect is a continuously changing non-stop scene with each new actor choosing his character and how he will react to the people left on stage.

A variation on I'm Sorry I Must Be Leaving is to start number one with an action, for example washing windows. When number two comes in, he takes number one's action but changes it slightly into something else, such as grooming a horse. Number one and number two then interact by number one joining in number two's activity until number three joins the action. Number one must now find an excuse to leave and number two must find a way of joining in number three's actions. Thus number three might now be conducting an orchestra so number two might pick up a violin and be conducted. It is important for the development of the game that the last person in is always in control of the scene.

Once again there is a fast-changing, free-flowing improvisation being played out for the audience. This is an excellent game with almost any group. If you feel a group might have problems with this activity, try Liar's Tag (the next game) as a starter. Obviously, for groups whose cognitive skills are slower than average, the game moves more slowly and may need more direction from the leader, *but* having played the game a couple of times, people slowly gain an awareness of the rules and create some fascinating scenes and scene changes.

Liar's Tag. The group sits in a circle. The leader starts miming an action, such as brushing his teeth. Number two, the person on his left, asks 'What are you doing?' The leader then has to lie, for example: 'I'm riding my bike.' Number two must then mime riding a bike. Number three then asks number two 'What are you doing?' The reply might be 'I'm taking a bath.' Number three must then mime taking a bath, and so on.

The person performing the action must tell the questioner a lie, and the questioner must then act out that lie. Again, this is an excellent game for most groups. For some groups with slower than average cognitive skills, time and patience must be allocated by the leader to allow the group to work at their own pace and within their own limitations.

Who Owned the Bag? This is a projective exercise and has many similarities to the Magic Box. I bring in a battered and aged bag. I have two I use regularly. One is an old-fashioned leather briefcase and the other is a hold-all made from alligator hide. I tell the group that it is a very old bag and has had many owners. I then ask the group to tell me who owned the bag. When someone tells me they know who owned the bag, I ask them to tell me about the owner. Normally the first piece of information is a job, e.g. 'It was owned by a doctor.' Once the group member has started to tell me about the owner I start asking questions, for example 'What's the owner's name?', 'How old is he?', 'How tall?', 'What colour is his hair?', 'How much does he weigh?', etc. Slowly, the person is building a physical picture of the bag's owner. Then I can start asking questions about the owner's lifestyle, the sort of house he lives in, his favourite foods, etc. Once I have done this with one person, then the group can be involved in asking subsequent informants about other owners of the bag.

In using a simple stimulus, an old bag, as a focal point, the group is able to create characters. These characters can be used in other exercises. Owners of the bag can act out the exchange of the bag from one to another. Scenes can be played with the bag's owner as the central character. The character can be used in a situation which is as yet unresolved by his creator, and so on.

The leader can always ask questions about the bag's owner which help the person describing him. If the description is very concrete, questions relating to emotion can be asked, such as 'How does he feel about his job?' If the description is very abstract, the leader can ask questions that 'anchor' the group member, for example 'What size of shoes does he wear?'

It is important to let the group member describing the bag's owner know that he is always right. He cannot say 'I think he is 5 feet 6 inches', for he is creating the character. The way the individual creates the character, the points he describes, the ones he avoids, particularly those dealing with the character's emotions, can be very valuable clues to completing the three-dimensional jigsaws I have spoken about throughout this chapter.

Postscript

In this chapter I have described some of the ways drama can be used with people to awaken the imagination, tell stories and create characters. I have tried to emphasise throughout the close link between imagination and dramatic action. Many groups are thought of as being incapable, unable to take part, and yet my experience is that in almost all cases this belief is unfounded. There are many with whom the process is a long, hard one *but* when the results occur, when someone is able to allow their imaginative thoughts to become action, to participate in dramatic activity, the wait and the effort all seem worthwhile.

In working with any group, the only real limits to an individual's taking part in dramatic activities are time, patience and the limits of the leader's imagination. It is within the power of the human imagination to overcome mental restrictions, physical limitations and emotional barriers, and, in so doing, truly to move mountains.

Acknowledgements

I wish to thank the following professional colleagues and friends for their advice, encouragement and inspiration over the years: Bill Morris, Dek Leverton, Gordi Wiseman, Sue Jennings, Derek Gale, Nancy Breitenbach, Tony Jeffries, Paul Johnson and Ian McHugh, and I must give special thanks to Derek Akers for all his help and advice; to Rob Watling, with whom I have shared so many of my successes and failures; and finally to Bert Amies, who is perhaps the single most important factor in my present way of working and in my current profession.

Notes

1. Bernard Beckerman, in *The Dynamics of Drama* suggested that drama occurs when 'one or more human beings, isolated in time and space, present themselves in imagined acts to another or others'. This definition, although primarily based on theatrical performance, does emphasise the importance both of the imagination and of communication between people.

2. Ritual is an extremely complicated concept, but at the risk of over-simplifying one can think of ritual as: consistently repeated actions (words, movements, sounds, expressions, etc.) that possess specific meaning for a particular group (tribe, subculture). Often rituals started as spontaneous random acts, which only later on acquired significance for other members of the group.

3. Do not confuse this loss of spontaneity with lack of meaning. It is when the group loses contact with, and understanding of, the purpose of the ritual that

the ritual loses meaning and becomes 'dead'. Refer to Rob Watling's chapter in this book.

4. Dramatic actions in this case could be viewed as speech or movement which is not simply functional but overly expressive or dramatic. Often these dramatic actions are socially unacceptable and are often exhibited by people who become our 'clients'.

5. Some basic books dealing with the concept of role are Erving Goffman's *Presentation of Self in Everyday Life* and Eric Berne's *Games People Play*. In addition, I would recommend Lyman and Scott's *Drama of Social Reality* and Elizabeth Burns's *Theatricality* to readers wishing to view these concepts in relation to drama/theatre.

6. Calibration relates to the mutual feedback process that all human beings are continually engaged in, in their attempts to communicate their feelings, beliefs, ideas, etc. to others. See David Gordon's *Therapeutic Metaphor*.

7. Richard Courtney, *The Dramatic Curriculum*.

8. Each individual's specific and personal way of viewing the world, which forms the basic grid by which all incoming stimuli are processed, categorised and stored.

9. Although I feel that we can transmit only on a single wavelength, I feel we are able to vary the quality and the intensity of the signal by careful choice of language and by the role we are in, in a similar way to adjusting the tone, volume and balance on a stereo.

10. Role-flexibility can be seen as both a change of 'social role', e.g. from husband to teacher to shopper to father to son, etc., but also it can be seen in terms of a change in 'social status' – dominant, equal or subordinate. In any set social role we may well be required to move status not only frequently but also rapidly during interactions with others. Role-flexibility is an essential skill for actors, but is also invaluable in facilitating everyday communication. I would recommend the book *Impro* by my colleague Keith Johnstone, to those interested in a slightly different perspective on status interactions in relation to theatre.

11. Role and character are frequently used interchangeably in the literature. However, when I speak of role-play, I am referring to improvised dramas created by the meeting and interaction of set role types, e.g. student and teacher, traffic cop and motorist. The responses of the types are left to the imaginations of the individuals playing the role, but are based on past experience and their general perceptions of that social role. However, the more information that is given about the role, e.g. name, age, favourite colour, gender, marital status, occupation of parents, etc., the closer one gets to a character with a known past history and probable emotional responses to any given situation. The greater the detail, the more the individual must respond 'as if' they were that character. This is in essence the basis of naturalistic acting.

12. Psychodrama, developed by Dr Jacob Moreno, is a term often used synonymously with drama therapy. Psychodrama and drama therapy, although they have many similarities and common roots, are *not* the same thing. For more details readers should refer to *Acting In* by Howard Blatner, and *Dramatherapy* vol. 3, no. 1 – an issue which is devoted to this topic.

13. Playing is integrally linked with dramatic activity. As my great friend and mentor, Bert Amies, often points out, whether children are playing 'cops and robbers' or even if you are playing Hamlet or Macbeth, it is still play – something that is often forgotten by some 'culture vultures'. See Callois' *Man, Play and Games* and Amies' 'New Games and Drama'.

14. The person leading a drama session can take many roles as leader, but in essence these are but facets of being a play leader – in the widest sense of the

term. However, there are three basic sub-roles that a play leader can assume. There is the role of the *actor* – where the leader is *actively* involved in the group and, apart from suggesting starting points, is almost totally non-directive. Then there is the role of *facilitator* – where the leader steps back a pace or two from the group in order that he may lend some objectivity. In this role the leader is *passively* guiding the group by asking questions, making observations that allow the group to make its own decisions and direction changes. Thirdly, there is the role of *director* – where the leader directs the group, providing a strong structure in which they must react and create. All play leaders exhibit a mixture of role types within their leadership style. Many switch roles as appropriate to the surroundings in which they work and to the people with whom they are interacting.

15. Activities that spotlight need to be set up so that they are non-threatening and supportive, so that those involved may gain a positive reinforcement of self-image and feel secure within the group's limelight.

16. Extra able-bodied helpers, whether volunteers or paid aides, can be a great help, but they can also be a pain in the —! Often, so much time is spent helping the helpers understand a particular way of working, or an individual's specific needs, that the moment is lost. However, sensitive or well-trained helpers who support those in greatest need without becoming too obtrusive can make the leader's job so much more simple. Volunteer help is essential when working with profoundly handicapped individuals, and a lot of my time is spent recruiting and educating voluntary help from janitors and kitchen staff as well as the more obvious professional colleagues and students.

17. As an example – in one session I was working with a young woman who had a cerebral palsy. As a manifestation of her condition she was unable to hold her head up for more than a minute or so at a time. She became so involved in the parachute activities that she maintained focus and control over her neck muscles and her head remained erect throughout the activity. Not only this, she was able to extend the reach in her arms way beyond their normal extension. Professionals who had worked with her remarked on the fact that they had never seen her so involved in an activity and commented that she was doing things they thought she was not capable of.

18. I strongly recommend readers interested in this area to refer to Bandler and Grinder's *The Structure of Magic*, Gordon's *Therapeutic Metaphors* and Watzlawick's *The Language of Change* for more detailed background information.

19. From the recording of the group's story a story book can be produced. This book can be used for people to read from. It can also be produced with large script and with lots of space between each word to allow the person to copy the word. This is not new educational practice, but the material the person is learning from has been created by them and this can affect the motivation to learn. Good results have been achieved using this method with adolescents from inner city areas who are street-wise but 'learning disabled'.

Suggested Reading and Films

Background to Drama and Drama Therapy

Beckerman, B. *The Dynamics of Drama* (Drama Book Specialists, New York, 1970)

Blatner, H. *Acting In* (Springer, Berlin, 1973)

Burns, E. *Theatricality* (Harper & Row, New York, 1973)

Courtney, R. *The Dramatic Curriculum* (Heinemann, London, 1980)

Jennings, S. *Remedial Drama* (Pitman, London, 1973)

Johnstone, K. *Impro* (Eyre Methuen, London, 1981)

Langley, D. with Langley, G. *Dramatherapy and Psychiatry* (Croom Helm, London, 1983)

Schattner, G. and Courtney, R. (eds) *Drama in Therapy*, 2 vols (Drama Book Specialists, New York, 1981)

Schechner, R. and Schuman, M. (eds) *Ritual, Play and Performance* (Seabury, New York, 1976)

Shaw, A., Perks, W. and Stevens, C.J. *Perspectives* (Drama and Theatre by, with and for Handicapped Individuals, Washington DC, 1981)

Way, B. *Development through Drama* (Longman, London, 1969)

Ideas/Activities

Barker, C. *Theatre Games* (Eyre Methuen, London, 1977)

Berne, E. *Games People Play* (Penguin, Harmondsworth, 1972)

Callois, R. *Man, Play and Games* (Thames & Hudson, London, 1962)

Spolin, V. *Improvisations for the Theatre* (Northwestern University Press, Evanston, 1963)

Films

'Breaking Free', Chris Noonan (director), 1981

'Feeling Good Feeling Proud', Richard Heus (director), 1981

MOVEMENT ANALYSIS *

The body is capable of a wide range of movement, but all movement can be broken down into five basic actions. This kind of breakdown is known as a 'movement analysis'.

The five basic actions are:

travel: redistribution of weight through space
balance: stillness in equilibrium
turn: rotation around an axis
jump: launching weight into the air
gesture: movement without change of weight

Further, the body is capable of three kinds of mechanical action: bending, stretching and twisting.

The quality of any movement can be described by four 'movement factors':

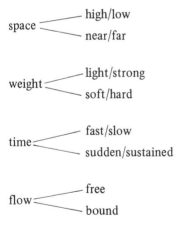

space ——— high/low
       ——— near/far

weight ——— light/strong
        ——— soft/hard

time ——— fast/slow
      ——— sudden/sustained

flow ——— free
      ——— bound

*Adapted from LUDUS Dance in Education Teachers' Pack for *The Thunder Tree,* eds C. Thomson and B. Warren

These actions and their movement factors can be described in many ways, as shown in the following table.

'How you move'					
Actions			Qualities		
hop	rock	stab	gentle	wide	lingering
skip	crawl	stroke	weak	small	dashing
step	slither	cut	heavy	tall	hurrying
run	twizzle	pinch	firm	thin	
bounce	wiggle	throw	long	fat	
leap	shake	catch	short	flat	
fall	carry	hold	angular	stiff	
stand	push	release	spiky	floppy	
rise	pull	wave	bendy	delicate	
roll	kick	flutter	curved	floating	
seesaw	punch	tense	rounded	flicking	

As well as these elements, all movements involve one or more *parts of the body*, have a *direction*, and are executed *in relation to* other people or objects.

In addition to the words that describe movement actions and qualities, here are some basic descriptors, which may be useful in planning, running or describing your sessions:

Body parts	Directions	Relationships
'What you move'	'Where you move'	'How or with whom'
whole body	up	with
head	down	against
neck	in	together
shoulders	out	copying
arms	backwards	contrasting
elbows	forwards	in pairs
wrists	in front	in threes, fours . . .
hands	behind	in groups
fingers	left	following
back	right	leading
hips	into the middle	joining
bottom	out to the side	leaving
tummy	straight	passing
legs	sideways	taking turns
knees	zig-zag	containing/enclosing
ankles	circle	
feet	spiral	
toes		
eyes		
mouth		
nose		

These ways of describing movement are fundamental to movement analysis. You can use movement analysis to help you recognise and note the movement capabilities of your group. For example, which parts of the body, if any, can they move in isolation? Can they travel? Balance? Can they travel, but only on the floor — i.e. roll, crawl — or can they travel only in a wheelchair?

Movement analysis, combined with your knowledge of the individual needs and capabilities of your group, will help you to decide on your movement aims and to structure the content of your sessions. In addition it enables you to describe and record an individual's 'behaviour' in movement terms, and to detail the changes that occur in your sessions over time.

CROSS-REFERENCE / ACTIVITIES INDEX

Presented below is an at-a-glance to the activities/materials discussed throughout this book. Alongside each activity is a checklist of the possible benefits that may result from participating in that activity. The reader is reminded that the specific outcomes of each activity will be dependent on the group, their leader and the contract between them. (Activities are marked in terms of their possible benefits with the major focus marked ✓ and the secondary outcomes marked ✗.)

ACTIVITIES ARE MARKED IN TERMS OF
THEIR POSSIBLE BENEFITS WITH
THE MAJOR FOCUS MARKED ✓
& THE SECONDARY OUTCOMES MARKED ✗

	1 BODY AWARENESS	2 FLEXIBILITY	3 COMMUNICATION SKILLS	4 ATTENTION SPAN/CONCENTRATION	5 EMOTIONAL RELEASE	6 IMAGINATION/CREATIVITY	7 SELF-ESTEEM/SELF-CONFIDENCE	8 GROUP COHESION/SOCIAL SKILLS	9 MOTOR SKILLS	10 PERCEPTION/SENSITIVITY		
ABSENT			✗	✗	✗			✓		✗	MUSIC	P.
ART/MUSIC	✗			✗	✗	✓	✗		✗	✗	ART	P.
BACKWARD BENDING	✗	✗✓					✗		✗	✗	ROOTS OF MVT	P.
BALL OF STRING			✗			✗	✗	✓		✗	MUSIC	P.
BIG BANG					✗	✗	✗	✓			MUSIC	P.
BLOCKS OF SOUND			✗✓							✗	MUSIC	P.

	1	2	3	4	5	6	7	8	9	10		
BODY BLUES	✓		X								MUSIC	P.
BREATH	X		X						✓		MUSIC	P.
BRUSHES		✓		X	X	X			✓		ART	P.
CALF STRETCHES	X			X	X	X	X		X	X	ROOTS OF MVT	P.
CALLING				X	X	✓		X	X	X	MUSIC	P.
CHANGE				X	X	X	✓	✓	X	✓	DANCE	P.
CHARCOAL				X	X	X	✓		X		ART	P.
CHORDS	✓		X						X	X	MUSIC	P.
COLLAGE			X	X	X	✓	X		X		ART	P.
CONTE				X	X	X	✓		✓		ART	P.
COURT DANCES				X	X	✓		✓	X		MUSIC	P.
CREATING IMAGERY THRU FANTASY			X	X	X	✓	X	X			ART	P.
CUMULATIVE GAMES			X	✓				X			FOLKLORE	P.
DANCE IN/DANCE OUT				✓	X	✓	X	X	X		DANCE	P.
DO THE OPPOSITE			X	X		X	✓	✓		X	FOLKLORE	P.
DRACULA			✓	X		X	✓				DRAMA	P.
DUPLET/TRIPLET	✓		✓	✓						✓	MUSIC	P.
ELECTRIC PUPPET		X		X					✓	X	DANCE	P.
ELEMENTS			X	X	✓	✓	X				MUSIC	P.
EVENTS			X		X	✓		X		X	MUSIC	P.
FEATHER DANCES	X			X					✓	X	DANCE	P.

Activity	1	2	3	4	5	6	7	8	9	10	Category	P.
FOOTBALL CHANT	X							X	X		MUSIC	P.
FRAMING		X	X	✓			✓	X	X	X	MUSIC	P.
GESTURES		✓	X				✓	X	X	X	MUSIC	P.
GOOD MORNING SIGNED			✓	X		X	X				MUSIC	P.
GROUNDING			X			X	X	✓			MUSIC	P.
GROUP TRUST/VISUAL ART					X	X	X	✓		X	ART	P.
GRUNTING		✓	X			✓	✓	X		X	MUSIC	P.
GUIDED FANTASY			X					X			DRAMA	P.
HAMSTRINGS	X	X			X	X	X		X	X	ROOTS OF MVT	P.
HANDS	X	✓	X			X	X		X	X	ROOTS OF MVT	P.
HELLO			X	✓			X	X			MUSIC	P.
HIP JOINTS/PELVIS	X	✓				X	X	X	X	X	ROOTS OF MVT	P.
HUMMING		X	✓			X	X	X	X		MUSIC	P.
I AM ME					✓	X	X	X	X		DANCE	P.
I'M SORRY I MUST BE LEAVING			X	X	✓	✓		X			DRAMA	P.
INK	X	✓			X	✓	X	✓	✓	X	ART	P.
INNER THIGHS	X	✓			X	X	X		X	X	ROOTS OF MVT	P.
JAPANESE SITTING POSITION	X		X			✓	X		X		ROOTS OF MVT	P.
KEENING	X	✓	X		✓				✓		MUSIC	P.
KEEPER OF THE KEYS			X	X					✓	✓	DRAMA	P.
LIARS TAG			X	X	✓						DRAMA	P.
LOIN/LOWER BACK STRETCH	X	✓	✓			X	X		X	X	ROOTS OF MVT	P.
LONDON			✓				X	X	✓		FOLKLORE	P.

	1	2	3	4	5	6	7	8	9	10		
MAGIC AURA	√								X	X √	DANCE	P.
MAGIC BOX			X							X	DRAMA	P.
MAGIC CLAY				X	√	√				X	DRAMA	P.
MAGIC NEWSPAPER			√	X		√	X				DRAMA	P.
MAJOR & MINOR	X							X			MUSIC	P.
MALE OR FEMALE ?								X		√	DRAMA	P.
MEMORY			X	√				√			MUSIC	P.
MINOR THIRD			X	X				√			MUSIC	P.
MIRRORS			X		X	√			X	√	MUSIC	P.
MIXED MEDIA					X		X		X		ART	P.
MR. ENGINE		X	X				X	√			DRAMA	P.
MUK			X	X	√						FOLKLORE	P.
MUSIC/DRAWING GAME											ART	P.
MUSIC/PHOTOGRAPHS/PAINTINGS	X			X	√				X		DANCE	P.
NAME CHORUS						X √	X	√			MUSIC	P.
NECK	X						X		X	X	ROOTS OF MVT	P.
NINJA	X	√			X				√	X	DANCE	P.
OCTAVE				√				X	√		MUSIC	P.
OH WHAT A BEAUTIFUL MORNING	X		X								MUSIC	P.
OIL PASTELS				X	X √	X			X		ART	P.
OPPOSITES			X	X	√					X	MUSIC	P.
ORGANUM			X	X				√			MUSIC	P.

	10	9	8	7	6	5	4	3	2	1		
ORNAMENTED FOLKSONG					✓			X		X	MUSIC	P
PAINT		X		X	✓	X	X	X			ART	P
PARACHUTE	X	✓	✓			X		X	✓		DRAMA	P
PARTNER TRUST/VISUAL ART	✓				X	X	X			X	ART	P
PASTELS		✓		X	✓	X	X				ART	P
PELVIS	X	X		X	X	X				X	ROOTS OF MVT	P
PENCILS(GRAPHITE)	✓	✓			X X	X	X				ART	P
PERCUSSIVE & SUSTAINED SONGS					✓					X X	MUSIC	P
PIANO QUINTET			X		✓	X		X		X X	MUSIC	P
PIG IN THE STY		✓	X	X	✓						FOLKLORE	P
PLAINSONG	X		X		✓						MUSIC	P
PULL THE BOAT	X	✓	✓	X	✓			X X		X	MUSIC	P
REED IN THE WIND	X	✓	✓	X		X				X	DANCE	P
RITUAL & THE THERAPY SESSION	✓	✓	✓	X					X	✓	FOLKLORE	P
ROB'S LITTLE FINGER GAME		✓	X						✓	✓	DANCE	P
ROCKETS	X			✓	✓			X		X	MUSIC	P
ROCKING - BACKWARDS/FORWARDS	✓	✓		X						X	MUSIC	P
ROCKING - SIDEWAYS	X	✓		X						X	MUSIC	P
SENTENCE			✓				X X				MUSIC	P
SHOULDERS	X X	X X		X					✓	X	ROOTS OF MVT	P
SHOULDER WORK IN PAIRS	X	X X	X						✓	X	ROOTS OF MVT	P
SIDE STRETCH	X	X	X	X					✓	X	ROOTS OF MVT	P

	1	2	3	4	5	6	7	8	9	10		
SILENT SONG							✗		✗	✓	MUSIC	P.
SIMPLE NAME GAME(S)		✓									DRAMA	P.
SOUND IMAGES			✗			✓	✓	✗			MUSIC	P.
SOUNDS STRUCTURED/FREE & SILENCE			✗			✓	✓	✗		✗	MUSIC	P.
SQUAT CALVES	✗						✗	✗	✗	✗	ROOTS OF MVT	P.
STAR POINTS			✗			✓		✗			MUSIC	P.
STAR RADIALS			✗			✓		✗	✓		MUSIC	P.
STEPPING STONES					✗	✗		✗			MUSIC	P.
STEREOPHONIC SOUND			✗		✗	✓		✗	✓	✗	MUSIC	P.
STICK IN THE MUD	✗					✗		✓		✗	FOLKLORE	P.
SUB DIVISION	✗							✓	✗		MUSIC	P.
SUN AND FROST			✓					✗	✗		FOLKLORE	P.
SUPPORT MUSIC						✓	✗	✗	✗		MUSIC	P.
TACTILE OBJECTS	✗	✓		✗	✗	✓	✗	✗		✗	MUSIC	P.
TAILOR POSITION	✗						✗	✗	✗		ROOTS OF MVT	P.
TARZAN	✓		✗				✓	✗			DRAMA	P.
TARZAN SONG	✗		✗	✗	✗						MUSIC	P.
TENNIS			✓	✗	✗			✗	✗	✗	MUSIC	P.
TENNIS/ELBOW/FOOT GAME			✗	✗				✗	✗		DRAMA	P.
THUMB FIFTHS			✗	✓				✗	✓		MUSIC	P.
TILE DANCE CHORUS			✗				✗				MUSIC	P.
TO BE CONTINUED			✗		✓			✗			DRAMA	P.

	1	2	3	4	5	6	7	8	9	10		
TOE SONG	✓		X					X			MUSIC	P
TOP THIGH STRETCH	X	✓		X	X	X	X		X	X	ROOTS OF MVT	P
TRADITIONAL NARRATIVES					X	X		✓			FOLKLORE	P
TRUNK ROTATIONS	X	X		X			X		X	X	ROOTS OF MVT	P
VOLLEY BALLOON		X		X				X	✓		DANCE	P
VOWELS			X		X	✓	X				MUSIC	P
WHO OWNED THE BAG ?		X	X	✓	X	✓	X	X		X	DRAMA	P
WITHIN THE INTERVAL			X					X			MUSIC	P

FURTHER READING

There follows a short and selective reading list. The books listed supplement those already recommended in previous chapters by individual contributing authors. Many of the books cited in this volume have their own extensive reading lists. For individuals wishing to delve further into the areas of arts therapy, creative therapy and personal creativity, the suggested reading represents no more than the tip of the iceberg. However, it does provide a springboard for further, more extensive background reading.

Alvin, J. *Music Therapy* (Basic Books, New York, 1975)

Bailey, P. *They Can Make Music* (Oxford University Press, Oxford, 1965)

Bandler, R. and Grinder, J. *The Structure of Magic*, 2 vols (Science and Behaviour Books, 1975/1976)

Bettelheim, B. *Freud and Man's Soul* (Alfred A. Knopf, New York, 1983)

Exley, H. *What It's Like to Be Me* (Exley, Watford, 1981)

Feder, E. and Feder, B. *The Expressive Arts Therapies* (Prentice-Hall, Hemel Hempstead, 1981)

Gaston, E.T. *Music in Therapy* (Macmillan, London/New York, 1968)

Goffman, E. *Presentation of Self in Everyday Life* (Penguin, Harmondsworth, 1978)

Gordon, D. *Therapeutic Metaphors* (Meta, Cupertine, California, 1978)

Haley, J. *Problem-solving Therapy* (Harper Colophon, New York, San Francisco and London, 1976)

Jennings, S. (ed.) *Creative Therapy* (Pitman, London, 1975)

Koestler, A. *The Act of Creation* (Hutchinson, London, 1976)

Lyman, S.M. and Scott, M.B. *Drama of Social Reality* (Oxford University Press, New York, 1975)

Michel, D.E. *Music Therapy: an Introduction to Therapy and Special Education through Music* (Charles C. Thomas, Springfield, Ill., 1976)

Shakespeare, R. *The Psychology of Handicap* (Methuen, London, 1975)

Sutherland, S. *Breakdown* (Granada, London, 1976)

Ward, D. *Music for Slow Learners* (Oxford University Press, Oxford, 1973)

Watzlawick, P. *The Language of Change* (Basic Books, New York, 1978)

INDEX